THE

Partytime

COOKBOOK

This edition is published with the permission of
HarperCollins Publishers Pty Limited.

Published in 1993 by
Tormont Publications Inc.
338 Saint Antoine St. East
Montreal, Canada H2Y 1A3
Tel. (514) 954-1441
Fax (514) 954-1443
ISBN 2-89429-389-5
Printed in Canada

Photography: David Levin
Food Styling: Elizabeth Carden

THE
Partytime
COOKBOOK

JANE ASPINWALL

JAN WUNDERLICH

TORMONT

Contents

Let's Have a Party!

Any reason for a party is a good reason. Whether you're celebrating a very special affair such as a wedding or anniversary in grand style, or simply in the mood for sharing a good time with those you care about, having a party is one of the best ways to socialize and enjoy life.

The art of entertaining well depends on planning and experience. If you're a first-time party giver, you'll probably have a few doubts about your organizational abilities. Don't fret, simply opt for an easy party outdoors such as a picnic or a barbecue, which involve a minimum of fuss and bother. Each time you entertain you'll gain more confidence until you can branch out into something more complicated. The experienced host might like more of a challenge, such as a fancy cocktail party or a formal dinner dance.

WHAT SORT OF PARTY CAN YOU AFFORD?

As with most things in life, the type and size of your party usually depends on your finances. When you set down your party budget, list all the expensive items such as food, drink, decorations and flowers, invitations, equipment rentals (chairs, glassware, cutlery, lighting, etc.) and proceed to eliminate those you can. If your mother, sister or next door neighbor has a particularly splendid garden full of blooms, they may let you select a few for decorative purposes, and you'll probably be able to borrow extra seating from friends and family.

Drawing up a guest list to suit your budget can be difficult. How do you possibly *not* invite one couple when you've decided to invite others? This is always a personal dilemma but if you're tactful and graceful, you shouldn't harm too many friendships. Consider scaling down other areas of

expense in order to accommodate an extra guest or two... often, it's the only real solution.

THE RIGHT MIX OF PEOPLE

What makes some parties buzz with excitement and fun while others tend to fizz out in unfulfilled expectations? Mostly, it's the blend of people that determines the life of the party. Too many talkers and not enough listeners can result in a loud and obnoxious group who are continually fighting for center stage, while a thoughtful bunch of philosophers will most likely spend the night mumbling into their beards! Mix interests, lifestyles and age groups till you have a marvellous medley from all walks of life – then watch the conversation crackle!

If you're an inexperienced host, do yourself a favor and avoid a large gathering; invite only those friends and family you feel comfortable with. If disaster does strike (and one day, dear reader, it will), at least with a team of friendly faces around you, you will be able to grin and bear it!

INVITATIONS

An informal party calls for little more than a quick telephone call or a casual mention at your next encounter. More formal occasions – weddings, engagements and christenings for example, will always call for a letter or invitation card. You can make these yourself if you have the time and creativity; your guests will be pleased with your extra thoughtfulness and find it an invitation hard to refuse. Make sure you specify all the vital information: date, time, address, type of party, attire (formal, informal, fancy dress or 'come as your are'), telephone number, reply address and an RSVP date. If you're holding the party at an unusual venue that may be unfamiliar to the guests, it's always wise to include a map or directions. Try to

issue mailed and telephone invitations on the same day, so that no one will feel they're an afterthought. And if you do suddenly remember someone you had left off the list, don't try to make excuses; just issue a casual 'Are you free on such-and-such for a little get-together I'm having?' Don't make a fuss and you'll be saved from embarrassment.

CHILDREN

Always be prepared for entertaining children. They usually don't want to be part of the adults' party so try to give them something amusing to do on their own. Videos and popcorn can be very useful.

If you have children of your own, ask friends to bring theirs along – this way you won't have to worry about your brood getting bored and your guests will save on babysitting costs.

Babies should be in a convenient bedroom away from the noise but near the parents, who'll probably spend all night popping in and out to check on them.

NEIGHBORS

People and parties inevitably mean noise – sometimes more noise than you had anticipated! Show your neighbors some consideration by observing noise pollution curfews if they apply in your neighborhood. Ask rowdy guests to move inside the house where more noise can be absorbed; issue guests with parking suggestions if street parking is a problem, and make sure they don't encroach on your neighbors' property. The best neighbor-taming method is to invite your immediate neighbors to join in – they may decline the invitation but appreciate it anyway.

CONSIDER A THEME

Consider special effects for both formal and casual occasions; you can go all the way and ask your guests to dress up appropriately, or simply use the theme as a way of linking food, music, lighting and venue. Possible themes might be Sixties, gangster, Western, jazz, any nationality, color (e.g. black and white), buffet, formal, beach, or picnic. If holding a costume party, make sure you give your guests plenty of time to invent their costumes. Remember, a theme gives people something to focus on; it can make planning easier for you and the party much more unusual and exciting for your guests.

MENU PLANNING

There's no need to spend hours in the kitchen in order to provide spectacular party fare: all you need is the right mix of food and a little care in its presentation. Visualize the food and drink you intend to serve as a painting – look for balance and harmony in color, taste and texture. Choose exciting and different ways to garnish plates and serving dishes as this can make all the difference to the 'eye appeal' of the food, no matter how tasty it is.

Your main guidelines for menu planning should be based on the occasion itself; what's good fare for one party may be inappropriate for another. Never experiment with new dishes on the day or night of the party – always stick with tried and true successes (but not the same dish over and over to the same guests, please!) or have a test run a week before. Combine interesting flavors and colors, and watch for too much soft or too much hard food served together.

PLAN AHEAD

Do try to make things easy for yourself by doing as much preparation ahead of time as possible. All-important mood setters like lighting and music should be thought about well in advance, leaving no room for last minute panic. Decorations such as flowers can be arranged the day before. Easy-to-prepare-and-serve foods will leave the host more relaxed and able to enjoy the occasion just as much as the guests. Many dishes can be frozen successfully, leaving only garnishes to be added. The better the planning, the greater your enjoyment will be.

Children's Party Checklist

★ Choose a location, time and theme, the more original, the better.

★ Send out interesting invitations two to three weeks ahead; try to keep the guest list small.

★ Choose the menu and do as much as possible ahead of time. (Check now if any guests have special dietary needs.)

★ Prepare house for the intended horde – clear away all valuables and establish 'off limits' boundaries such as bedrooms, studies, etc.

★ Ensure that all children can be delivered and picked up at the designated times; have a list of contact numbers for parents in case of emergency or illness.

★ Ask another adult to help out and give you support for the afternoon. You'll need it!

★ Decorate party area with balloons, streamers and posters, anything that's bright and cheery.

★ Give the children plenty of room to move and make a mess; preferably outdoors.

★ Have on hand a good supply of prizes, at least one for every child. Extras may come in handy in case of tantrums!

★ Be sure your home and yard are safe for party activities; inform your neighbors of the event so they can keep a lookout for 'escapees' and wanderers!

★ Keep pets away from the party zone; they may frighten timid guests or tempt little terrors!

★ Arrange a set of rainy-weather alternative games and activities.

★ Assemble goodie bags as far ahead of time as possible; make a few spares for last-minute arrivals and some for brothers and sisters.

Apple Bobbing: Best as an outdoor activity, fill large tubs or buckets with water, place whole or halved apples in the water and challenge children to retrieve the apples using teeth only. Sure to cause a few splashes but lots of fun!

Musical Statues: A variation on the musical chairs theme, each guest must dance and move about while the music is played; when it stops suddenly, each must freeze perfectly still. Those who fail to do so are eliminated until there's a final winner.

Treasure Hunt: With secret little treasures hidden throughout the house and garden, issue each guest a clue that leads them to the next clue, and the next, until eventually they uncover the booty. Small amounts of coin money are always well-received!

Eat The Ice Cream: Watch how fast children consume the prize in this game! You'll need a hat, gloves, sunglasses, large apron and a pair of large boots plus a big bowl of ice cream and the smallest spoon you can find. Place all this in the middle of a circle of children and give them a couple of dice. Each child takes turns at rolling the dice until someone lands a six; the winner then leaps into the middle of the circle, puts on all the clothing then begins to eat the ice cream using the spoon. Meanwhile, the other players continue to roll the dice until another six is thrown. The winner then assumes the ice cream-eating role, even if the previous winner has only just managed to put on the gloves! It's frenzied fun in a mad race for just one bite of the ice cream!

Special Celebrations

Fabulous food for those special occasions whether dressed up or a casual get-together – anniversaries, birthdays to remember, engagements, weddings, christenings, game victories or simply time to have a party. These recipes have been chosen to impress guests while being easy to prepare and serve for buffets, cocktail parties or even sit-down affairs.

Savory Starters

GUACAMOLE

4 ripe avocados
juice of 2 lemons or limes
1 tsp (5 mL) salt (optional)
2 large onions, grated
2 cloves garlic, crushed
2 tsp (10 mL) curry powder
pinch cayenne
few drops Tabasco sauce (optional)
chopped red chili peppers, to garnish
taco or corn chips, to serve

Mash avocados with fork or blend in food processor. Add lemon juice and salt. Add remaining ingredients to avocado. Cover with plastic wrap and chill to serve. Spoon into 2 bowls before serving. Garnish with chopped red chili peppers. Serve with taco chips and vegetable sticks.
Note: For this versatile Mexican dish, look for very ripe avocados. If preparing in advance, mash avocados with a wooden spoon and store the finished guacamole in a jar with the avocado pits. This will prevent discoloring.

Makes 4 cups (1 L)

CHICKEN LIVER PATÉ

2 lbs (1 kg) chicken livers
¾ cup (185 mL) butter
2 cloves garlic, crushed
5 tbsp (75 mL) dry sherry
6 tbsp (90 mL) brandy
1 tbsp (15 mL) chopped parsley
½ tsp (2.5 mL) chopped fresh thyme
pinch cinnamon
pinch grated nutmeg
salt and freshly ground pepper, to taste
¼ cup (60 mL) whipping cream

Clean chicken livers. Heat 6 tbsp (90 mL) butter, add garlic and cook for 30 seconds. Add chicken livers and cook for 5 minutes or until almost cooked. Purée chicken livers and cooking liquid in food processor or blender. Put in bowl.

Heat remaining butter. Add remaining ingredients except cream and heat through. Pour over chicken livers and beat well. Stir in cream, taste and adjust seasoning. Spoon mixture into a serving container, cover and chill. Serve with crackers.

Serves 10–12

HOT DIP FOR RAW VEGETABLES

5 cloves garlic
3 tbsp (45 mL) milk
1¼ cups (310 mL) olive oil
4 tbsp (60 mL) butter
4 oz (110 g) anchovies, finely chopped

Chop garlic very finely and leave it in the milk for a few hours to remove some of its pungency. Put oil and butter in a heatproof earthenware pot, add anchovies and drained garlic and cook on very low heat for about 15 minutes, stirring from time to time. Serve immediately, with prepared vegetables.

Serves 4

Raw Vegetables with Hot Dip and Canapés

COUNTRY COMBINATION PATÉ

1 onion, chopped
1 clove garlic, crushed
sprig fresh thyme
sprig parsley
sprig fresh chervil
¼ cup (60 mL) butter
½ lb (225 g) chicken livers, cleaned
salt and pepper, to taste
¼ lb (110 g) fat pork, roughly chopped
¼ lb (110 g) lean pork, roughly chopped
6 slices bacon

Gently cook onion, garlic and herbs in butter for 1–2 minutes, then add livers diced into ¾ inch (2 cm) pieces, and cook gently for about 1 minute. Cool, then season and purée with pork.

Line a loaf pan with bacon slices and spoon in meat mixture, covering it with more slices of bacon. Stand pan in a baking dish half-full of water and bake at 350°F (180°C) for 1 hour. Cool, then refrigerate until firm. When chilled, slice paté and serve on lettuce leaves, accompanied by triangles of toast.

Serves 8

SMOKED FISH PATÉ

4 smoked mackerel fillets *or* 2 whole smoked mackerel
juice of 2 limes *or* 1 lemon
4 oz (110 g) cream cheese, softened
½ lb (225 g) butter, melted
pepper, to taste
sprigs of fresh herbs such as dill, fennel, flat-leaf parsley
lemon slices, to garnish
Melba toast or crackers, to serve

Skin and flake mackerel. Place in a blender or food processor with lime juice, cream cheese and butter. Blend to a purée. Season with pepper.

Turn into a suitable size serving dish and chill for several hours. Garnish with fresh herbs and lemon slices.

Serve with Melba toast or crackers.

Serves 4–6

TARAMASALATA

2 slices stale whole-wheat bread
2½ oz (75 g) smoked cod roe
1 clove garlic, crushed
pinch cayenne pepper
juice of 1–2 lemons
paprika, to taste
⅔ cup (165 mL) olive oil

Remove crusts from bread and soak slices in a little water. Remove skins from cod roe and pound to a smooth paste. Squeeze bread dry and add to roe with garlic and cayenne pepper. Continue to pound mixture until it is really smooth. Gradually stir in lemon juice and oil and beat vigorously. Transfer to serving dish, sprinkle with paprika and serve with toast.
Note: All ingredients can be put in a blender or food processor and blended until smooth.

Serves 4

OYSTER CHEESE PUFFS

¼ lb (110 g) butter
1½ cups (375 mL) grated sharp cheddar cheese
2 tsp (10 mL) sherry
1 egg, separated
2 x 4 oz (110 g) cans smoked oysters, drained
32 x 1½ inch (4 cm) bread rounds
1 tbsp (15 mL) finely chopped parsley
paprika, to taste

Beat butter, cheese and sherry together. Add egg yolk and blend well. Whisk egg white till soft peaks form. Fold egg white into cheese mixture.

Place 1 oyster on each round of bread. Top with 1 tsp (5 ml) of cheese mixture. Sprinkle with chopped parsley and paprika. Place on baking sheets. Bake at 450°F (230°C) for 10 minutes and serve piping hot.

Makes 32

CRUNCHY CHICKEN LIVERS WITH SOUR CREAM DIP

oil, for deep-frying
⅓ cup (85 mL) cornmeal
¼ cup (60 mL) all-purpose flour, sifted
½ tsp (2.5 mL) salt
½ tsp (2.5 mL) garlic salt
pinch pepper
1 egg
3 tbsp (45 mL) milk
7 chicken livers, cleaned and cut into ¾ inch (2 cm) pieces

SOUR CREAM DIP
1 cup (250 mL) sour cream
3 tbsp (45 mL) grated onion
½ tsp (2.5 mL) salt
¼ tsp (1 mL) Worcestershire sauce
1 tsp (5 mL) Dijon mustard
4 drops Tabasco *or* chili pepper sauce

Combine all dip ingredients, cover and refrigerate until ready to serve.

Put 1½ inch (3.5 cm) oil in an electric frying pan or deep fryer. Carefully heat oil to 375°F (190°C) while preparing chicken livers.

Combine cornmeal, flour and seasonings. Mix egg with milk. Dip each piece of liver into seasoned cornmeal, then into egg mixture and then into cornmeal again.

Deep-fry for 2 minutes or until golden brown. Serve hot on toothpicks with dip.
Note: These appetizers can be prepared in advance. To reheat livers place in a 350°F (180°C) oven for about 10 minutes.

Makes about 30 appetizers and 1 cup (250 mL) dip

SMOKED SALMON QUICHE

PASTRY
2 cups (500 mL) all-purpose flour
salt, to taste
¼ lb (110 g) butter
4–5 tbsp (60–75 mL) cold water

FILLING
6 oz (180 g) smoked salmon
4 egg yolks, beaten
4 whole eggs, beaten
1¼ cups (310 mL) sour cream
3 tbsp (45 mL) lemon juice
¾ cup (185 mL) light cream
½ tsp (2.5 mL) cayenne pepper
freshly ground pepper
½ cup (125 mL) grated Swiss cheese

Preheat oven to 400°F (200°C). Sift flour and salt into a bowl. Work in butter till mixture resembles breadcrumbs. Add sufficient water to form a soft dough. Knead lightly on floured board. Roll out dough to fit 8 inch (20 cm) quiche pan. Prick base of crust with fork. Bake pastry crust for 10 minutes.

Layer salmon in pastry crust. Blend egg yolks, eggs, sour cream, lemon juice, cream, cayenne and black pepper. Strain and pour into pastry crust. Top with grated cheese.

Bake at 375°F (190°C) for 45–60 minutes or until set and browned on top. Cut into slices and serve hot or cold.

Serves 12–16

Left to right: Country Combination Paté and Smoked Fish Paté

A selection of party canapés

CANAPÉS

Canapés provide a bite-sized starter to any party. Remove crusts from white, whole-wheat or rye bread. Toast or pan-fry bread slices to brown both sides. Cut bread slices into 1 inch (2.5 cm) squares, or use a small cookie cutter to cut bread into shapes. Allow toasted bread shapes to cool.

Cheese pastry shapes can be made as an alternative to bread shapes. Make a quantity of cheese pastry, roll out thinly, cut into various shapes and bake. A variety of savory crackers can also be used.

TASTY TOPPINGS

SPICY SARDINE
4 tbsp (60 mL) butter
1½ tsp (7.5 mL) lemon juice
1½ tsp (7.5 mL) prepared mustard
sardines and pimiento, to garnish

Combine first three ingredients to make lemon-mustard butter and spread toast or crackers with mixture. Top with ½ sardine and a thin strip of pimiento.

Makes ⅓ cup (85 mL)

SMOKED OYSTER OR MUSSEL
1 quantity lemon-mustard butter
  (see above recipe)
4 oz (110 g) can smoked oysters *or* mussels
finely chopped parsley, to garnish

Butter toast as for Spicy Sardine Canapés. Top each with a smoked oyster or mussel. Sprinkle with finely chopped parsley.

CREAM CHEESE
8 oz (225 g) cream cheese, softened
4 oz (110 g) can drained, smoked oysters *or*
¼ cup (60 mL) finely chopped pecans and pinch cayenne pepper *or*
¼ cup (60 mL) finely chopped chicken *and* pinch dry mustard *and* 1 tbsp (15 mL) chopped parsley
parsley, fresh herbs or watercress, to garnish

Combine ingredients, spread on toast rounds or crackers and garnish.

Makes approximately 1¼ cups (310 mL)

FILO DELIGHTS

12 oz (340 g) package filo pastry
½ lb (225 g) butter, melted

SEAFOOD FILLING
¼ cup (60 mL) cottage cheese
8 oz (225 g) can crabmeat, drained
2 green onions, chopped
salt and pepper, to taste

SPINACH CHEESE FILLING
4 oz (110 g) spinach, shredded and cooked
1 small onion, chopped
1 oz (28 g) feta cheese, crumbled
½ tsp (2.5 mL) lemon juice
pepper, to taste

CHILI PEPPER MEAT FILLING
¼ lb (110 g) cooked ground beef
1 tbsp (15 mL) chili pepper sauce or to taste
1 small onion, chopped

CREAM CHEESE FILLING
4 oz (110 g) cream cheese, softened
2 green onions, chopped
salt and pepper, to taste

To prepare the fillings, combine ingredients, adjusting seasoning as necessary.

Place pastry between 2 dry dish towels and cover with a barely damp dish towel. Take 2 sheets of pastry at a time and place 1 on top of the other. Cut pastry into 6 pieces, across the width. Brush each piece of pastry with a little butter.

Place 1 tsp (5 mL) of selected filling in left-hand corner of pastry piece. Fold other corner of pastry up to cover filling to form a large triangle. Fold left-hand corner up to form a smaller triangle. Continue folding in corners to make a neat package of the filling. Brush with melted butter. Repeat with remaining pastry and filling.

Place on baking tray. Bake at 400°F (200°C) for 15–20 minutes until golden brown. Serve hot.
Note: Filo Delights can be filled in advance. Layer uncooked triangles between sheets of plastic wrap and freeze for up to 2 weeks. Place frozen into hot oven to cook and brown.

Makes approximately 50

SHRIMP AND CHEESE TARTS

PASTRY
1½ cups (375 mL) all-purpose flour
pinch salt
¼ lb (110 g) butter
½ cup (125 mL) grated cheese
3 tbsp (45 mL) cold water

FILLING
½ cup (125 mL) chopped cooked shrimp
1 cup (250 mL) grated aged cheddar
1 tbsp (15 mL) chopped leek
4 eggs
½ cup (125 mL) cream
½ cup (125 mL) milk
pinch dry mustard
grated rind of 1 lemon
salt and pepper, to taste

Preheat oven to 375°F (190°C). Sift flour and salt into a bowl. Rub in butter till mixture resembles breadcrumbs. Mix in cheese and sufficient water to form a soft dough. Knead lightly on floured board. Roll out thinly and cut into 24 x 2½ inch (6 cm) rounds to fit tart tins.

Press pastry gently into base of tins. Place small amount of chopped shrimp in bottom of pastry. Top with portion each of cheese and leek. Blend together eggs, cream, milk, mustard, lemon rind, salt and pepper. Spoon egg mixture over shrimp and cheese.

Bake pies at 375°F (190°C) for 15–20 minutes or until golden and puffy. Serve hot or cold.

Makes 24

Left to right: Filo Delights and Shrimp and Cheese Tarts

HAM AND MUSHROOM PASTRIES

4 sheets frozen store-bought puff
    pastry, thawed
1 egg, beaten

FILLING
¼ lb (110 g) ham, diced
1 onion, chopped
1½ cups (375 mL) mushrooms, sliced
2 tbsp (30 mL) butter
1 stick celery, chopped
1 tbsp (15 mL) chopped parsley
2 tsp (10 mL) tomato purée or paste
pepper, to taste

Fry ham, onion and mushrooms in butter until onion is transparent. Add celery, parsley, tomato purée and pepper. Heat until liquid has evaporated. Remove from heat and cool.

Cut pastry sheets into 9 rounds, using a 4 inch (10 cm) cutter. Place 1 heaping tbsp (20 mL) of mixture on one half of each round. Fold over pastry to form half-moon shape. Press edges together to seal, and use tines of a fork to make crimped edge. Brush with beaten egg.

Place pastries on baking sheet. Bake at 425°F (220°C) for 15–20 minutes. Serve hot or cold.

Makes 36

SMOKED FISH CREAMS

⅔ lb (300 g) smoked haddock fillets
salt and freshly ground pepper, to
    taste
freshly grated nutmeg, to taste
2 eggs, beaten
1 cup (250 mL) whipping cream
sprigs fresh dill, to garnish

Carefully skin fish and cut into pieces. Place in an electric blender with herbs and blend to a smooth purée. Blend in eggs and transfer mixture to a bowl. Cover and refrigerate overnight.

Preheat oven to 375°F (190°C). Fill a large roasting pan with about 1 inch (2.5 cm) boiling water and place in center of oven. Return fish mixture to blender with cream and blend thoroughly. Lightly grease 8 x 3¼ inch (6 cm) ramekins and fill them three-quarters full with mixture. Place ramekins in roasting pan containing ½ inch (1 cm) water and bake for 30 minutes.

Serve creams immediately, either in ramekins or turned out onto plates. Garnish with fresh dill.

Serves 8

The Main Meal

CREAMY CRAYFISH CURRY

5 tbsp (75 mL) butter
1 small onion, finely chopped
1 green apple, peeled, cored and
    chopped
12 peppercorns
⅓ cup (85 mL) all-purpose flour
2½ tsp (12.5 mL) curry powder
1 bay leaf
pinch nutmeg
2½ cups (625 mL) milk
2 tsp (10 mL) lemon juice
½ tsp (2.5 mL) Worcestershire sauce
extra 4 tbsp (60 mL) butter
1¾ lbs (800 g) uncooked crayfish or
    lobster meat, chopped
¼ cup (60 mL) cream
3 tbsp (45 mL) sherry
1 tbsp (15 mL) finely chopped parsley,
    to garnish

OPTIONAL ADDITIONS
1½ tbsp (20 mL) butter
1 cup (250 mL) diced carrot
1 cup (250 mL) frozen peas
1 red or green pepper, diced
1 cup (250 mL) button mushrooms

In a saucepan, heat butter and sauté onion, apple and peppercorns over medium heat until onion is transparent. Add flour, curry powder, bay leaf, and nutmeg and cook for 1 minute. Stir in milk, lemon juice and Worcestershire sauce. Bring slowly to boil and simmer until mixture thickens, stirring continually. Cook 1–2 minutes longer, taste and adjust seasoning.

Strain sauce through a fine sieve, pressing vegetables against sieve to extract all sauce.

Melt extra butter in frying pan. Sauté crayfish meat for 3 minutes. Remove from heat and set aside. Sauté any optional additions in the optional butter and combine with curry sauce, cream and sherry. Gently heat through and fold in crayfish meat. Simmer for 2 minutes. Spoon curry into serving dish. Sprinkle with chopped parsley.

Serves 6

CURRY VARIATIONS

SHRIMP CURRY
Replace crayfish meat with
1½ lb (675 g) peeled uncooked shrimp

Serves 6

CHICKEN CURRY
Replace crayfish meat with
1¾ lbs (800 g) diced chicken meat or
3 lbs (1.5 kg) chicken pieces

Serves 6

PARTY CRAB CRÊPES

16–18 crêpes (see recipe page 46)

FILLING
1½ tbsp (20 mL) butter
6 mushrooms, sliced
3 tbsp (45 mL) finely chopped onion
½ lb (225 g) canned crabmeat, drained
1½ tbsp (20 mL) extra butter
⅓ cup (85 mL) all-purpose flour
½ tsp (2.5 mL) rosemary
salt and pepper, to taste
1½ cups (375 mL) chicken stock
1½ cups (375 mL) sour cream
1 tbsp (15 mL) chopped parsley
1 cup (250 mL) grated Swiss cheese
paprika, to taste
parsley, to garnish

To prepare filling, melt butter in frying pan. Add mushrooms and onion and sauté 3 minutes. Add crabmeat, remove pan from heat.

Melt extra butter in another saucepan. Add flour, rosemary, salt and pepper and cook, stirring constantly, for 3 minutes. Gradually stir in chicken stock, bring to a boil and cook for 3 minutes. Add sour cream, parsley and ½ cup (125 mL) Swiss cheese. Fold in crab mixture and stir until heated through.

Allow to cool slightly. Place ¼ cup (60 mL) filling along center of each crêpe and roll up. Arrange fold-side down in a single layer in a baking dish. Top with remaining cheese and sprinkle with paprika. Heat in oven at 350°F (180°C) for 10–15 minutes. Garnish with parsley to serve.

Serves 5–6

Party Crab Crêpes (above) and Creamy Crayfish Curry (below)

ROAST FRUITED DUCK WITH APRICOT CITRUS SAUCE

5 lb (2.5 kg) duck
2 cloves garlic, crushed
2 cups (500 mL) grated apple
12 pitted prunes
5 tbsp (75 mL) breadcrumbs
1 egg
3 tbsp (45 mL) brown sugar
salt and pepper, to taste

APRICOT CITRUS SAUCE
16 oz (450 g) can apricots, drained
    and chopped
½ cup (125 mL) white wine
juice and finely grated rind of
    1 orange
½ small onion, finely chopped

Preheat oven to 350°F (180°C). Wash duck and remove oil sacks from tail. Dry duck with paper towels and prick back several times with a skewer. Combine remaining ingredients and fill cavity with mixture. Secure opening with skewer.

Place duck on roasting rack in baking dish. Cook for 1 hour covered with lid or aluminum foil. Remove cover and roast additional 30–40 minutes. Cover and allow duck to stand 15 minutes before carving. Serve hot or cold.

To make sauce, combine all ingredients in pan, bring to a boil then reduce heat and simmer 10 minutes. Pour into a gravy boat and serve.

Serves 6

CHICKEN WITH PLUM AND LYCHEE SAUCE

3 lb (1.5 kg) chicken, cut in bite-size
    pieces
1 clove garlic, crushed
1 tsp (5 mL) finely chopped ginger
1 tbsp (15 mL) soy sauce
½ cup (125 mL) Chinese plum sauce
¼ tsp (1 mL) chili pepper sauce
1 tbsp (15 mL) vegetable oil
¼ cup (60 mL) water chestnuts
¼ cup (60 mL) bamboo shoots, sliced
½ lb (225 g) can lychees, drained
¼ cup (60 mL) canned lychee juice
3 tbsp (45 mL) cornstarch
1 tsp (5 mL) sesame oil

Remove skin from chicken pieces. Marinate for 2 hours with garlic, ginger, soy, plum and chili pepper sauces. Drain and reserve liquid. Add vegetable oil to wok, heat and stir-fry chicken pieces; cover with lid and simmer 5 minutes.

Add marinade juices. Cover and cook further 5 minutes. Add water chestnuts, bamboo shoots and lychees and stir-fry 1–2 minutes. Combine lychee juice and cornstarch, add to wok and heat until thickened. Stir in sesame oil and serve hot with steamed rice.

Serves 6

SUMMER CHICKEN WITH CREAM AND TARRAGON SAUCE

3 lb (1.5 kg) chicken
4 tbsp (60 mL) butter
2 tsp (10 mL) tarragon
juice of 1 lemon
3 carrots, peeled and roughly
    chopped
1 onion, peeled and halved
1 bouquet garni (*see glossary*)
3 tbsp (45 mL) dry vermouth
4 egg yolks
½ cup (125 mL) cream
salt and pepper, to taste
1 tbsp (15 mL) Madeira wine
tarragon sprigs, to garnish

Rinse chicken with cold water and pat dry using paper towels. Beat together butter and tarragon until smooth and rub inside chicken cavity and just under skin. Rub lemon juice all over chicken. Place chicken in a large saucepan with carrots, onion, bouquet garni and dry vermouth. Add sufficient water to cover chicken. Place over medium heat. Cover and simmer 1½ to 1¾ hours. Remove chicken and place on a large plate to cool for 20 minutes, then carve into large portions and remove skin.

Skim as much fat as possible from top of cooking liquid. Measure out 2 cups (500 mL) of cooking liquid, gradually add combined egg yolks and cream and beat well. Place in a double boiler and cook, stirring constantly until thickened. Season to taste and add Madeira.

Arrange chicken in a single layer in a shallow dish and spoon over sauce. Garnish with sprigs of fresh tarragon and refrigerate for at least 1 hour before serving.

Serves 6

Roast Fruited Duck with Apricot Citrus Sauce (above) and Chicken with Plum and Lychee Sauce (below)

Left to right: Fillets of Fish in Sangria Sauce and Stir-Fried Beef and Mushrooms

FILLETS OF FISH IN SANGRIA SAUCE

12 white fish fillets
½ cup (125 mL) all-purpose flour
salt and pepper, to taste
3 tbsp (45 mL) lemon juice
4 tbsp (60 mL) butter
juice of ½ orange
1 tbsp (15 mL) grated orange zest
¼ cup (60 mL) rosé or white wine
2 egg yolks, beaten
cayenne pepper, to taste
¼ cup (60 mL) cream
1 tbsp (15 mL) chopped parsley
1 tsp (5 mL) extra butter
peel from 1 orange, cut in fine strips and blanched

Coat fish fillets in combined flour, salt and pepper. Combine half the lemon juice and half the butter in frying pan. Heat till butter melts. Fry 6 fish fillets, 2 minutes on each side. Set fish fillets aside on platter. Drain juices from pan. Heat remaining lemon juice and butter and fry remaining fish fillets. When cooked, place on serving platter, cover with aluminum foil and keep warm in oven.

Combine orange juice, zest and white wine in top of double boiler. Bring to boil, then reduce heat to simmer. Add egg yolks and cayenne, stirring until thickened. Remove pan from heat.

Stir in cream, parsley and butter. Pour sauce over fish fillets and serve garnished with orange strips.

Serves 6

STIR-FRIED BEEF AND MUSHROOMS

5 dried Chinese mushrooms
1 lb (450 g) round steak, cut in slivers across the grain
2 cloves garlic, crushed
¼ tsp (1 mL) chopped fresh ginger
1 tbsp (15 mL) soy sauce
3 tbsp (45 mL) oyster sauce
1 tbsp (15 mL) vegetable oil
¼ lb (110 g) snow peas
2 stalks celery, sliced
3 handfuls spinach leaves, shredded
1 tsp (5 mL) sesame oil

Soak mushrooms in hot water for 20 minutes. Drain and discard stalks.

Combine steak, garlic, ginger, soy and oyster sauces. Marinate for 1 hour, drain and reserve liquid.

Heat vegetable oil in wok, add beef and fry till browned. Add marinade juices, fry for 3–5 minutes. Add mushrooms and cook for 2 minutes. Add snow peas and celery and fry 1 minute. Serve hot on spinach and sprinkle with sesame oil.

Serves 6

SLICED BEEF PLATTER WITH GREEN SAUCE

2–3 lb (1–1.5 kg) fillet of beef
salt and freshly ground pepper
⅓ cup (85 mL) butter
¼ cup (60 mL) brandy
1 cup (250 mL) beef consommé
3 tbsp (45 mL) sherry
1 tbsp (15 mL) gelatine
¼ lb (110 g) ham
1 tbsp (15 mL) mayonnaise
pinch cayenne

GREEN SAUCE
¼ cup (60 mL) finely chopped
    watercress
¼ cup (60 mL) finely chopped parsley
1 clove garlic, crushed
freshly ground pepper
4 capers, finely chopped
¼ cup (60 mL) olive oil
juice of 1 lemon
salt, to taste

Trim fillet, remove all skin and tissue with a sharp knife. Rub meat with salt and pepper.

Melt butter in shallow pan. Sauté fillet for 10 minutes or until brown on all sides. Warm brandy, pour over beef fillet and ignite. Cook until flame dies down.

Place fillet in a shallow roasting pan. Pour pan juices on top. Roast at 400°F (200°C) for 15–20 minutes. Allow beef to cool. Chill in refrigerator.

Place consommé, sherry and gelatine in saucepan and bring to a boil. Boil for 5 minutes. Remove ¾ cup (185 mL) of consommé mixture and set aside. Pour remaining consommé into shallow pan. Chill to set.

Purée ham till smooth. Fold in mayonnaise and cayenne. Spread cold beef with ham paste.

Spoon reserved consommé glaze over beef. Chill well. Slice beef carefully and arrange slices on platter. Chop up chilled set glaze and spoon around beef fillet. Serve with Green Sauce.

To make Green Sauce, combine watercress, parsley, garlic, pepper and capers in a small bowl. Add oil, drop by drop, beating constantly. Gradually add lemon juice and taste to adjust seasonings. Store in refrigerator in a screw-top jar until ready to serve.

Serves 8

SHREDDED BARBECUE DUCK

4½ lb (2 kg) duck
1 clove garlic, crushed
1 tbsp (15 mL) sesame oil
1 tbsp (15 mL) honey
1 tbsp (15 mL) hoisin sauce
1 tbsp (15 mL) soy sauce
1 tsp (5 mL) chili pepper sauce

BARBECUE SAUCE
½ tsp (2.5 mL) finely grated fresh
    ginger
1 tbsp (15 mL) light soy sauce
1 tbsp (15 mL) honey
1 tbsp (15 mL) dry sherry
1 tbsp (15 mL) hoisin sauce

Preheat oven to 375°F (190°C). Clean duck and dry with paper towels. Combine garlic, sesame oil, honey, hoisin, soy and chili pepper sauces. Brush marinade over duck.

Place duck on rack in baking dish. Cover with aluminum foil and bake 1 hour, brushing occasionally with marinade. Remove foil, and bake a further 30–40 minutes or until cooked. Juices should run clear when thigh is pricked with a skewer.

Allow duck to stand 15 minutes before slicing into thin strips. Separate the legs and wings at the joints. Serve duck arranged in layers on platter with wings and legs at end of platter. Serve hot or cold. To make sauce, combine all ingredients in a pan, heat through and serve in a gravy boat.

Serves 6

PORK AND PINEAPPLE HOTPOT

4 tbsp (60 mL) butter
3 lb (1.5 kg) pork fillet, diced
1 cup (250 mL) canned pineapple
    pieces, drained
2 green peppers, seeded
1 cup (250 mL) chopped celery
1 cup (250 mL) canned mushrooms,
    drained
1 red chili pepper, diced
1 cup (250 mL) white wine
salt and pepper, to taste
1 cup (250 mL) chicken stock
4 tbsp (60 mL) cornstarch
3 tbsp (45 mL) chopped parsley

Melt butter in a large saucepan, add pork and cook 10 minutes, turning constantly. Add pineapple, green pepper, celery, mushrooms and chili pepper. Cook 1 minute, stirring to combine. Add wine, salt and pepper and simmer 20 minutes. In a separate bowl combine stock, cornstarch and parsley. Add to pan and cook over medium heat 10 minutes, stirring occasionally. Serve with boiled rice.

Serves 6

VEAL WITH TUNA SAUCE

2½ lb (1.2 kg) veal (a boned piece
    of leg is ideal)
1 carrot
1 onion
2 celery stalks
1 strip lemon or orange peel
⅔ cup (165 mL) white wine
⅔ cup (165 mL) olive oil
salt, to taste
7 oz (200 g) can tuna in oil
4 anchovy fillets
1½ cups (375 mL) homemade
    mayonnaise
1 tbsp (15 mL) capers
3 stuffed olives

Roll up meat and secure with string or toothpicks to maintain its shape. Place it in a deep casserole or pan with carrot, onion, celery, a strip of lemon peel, wine, olive oil and 1¼ cups (310 mL) cold water. Salt lightly and cook in the oven or on top of the stove for 1 hour or until veal is done. Lift it out and allow to cool.

Strain cooking liquid and reduce it over high heat until well concentrated. Place tuna with its oil in a food processor, together with a little of the reduced cooking broth and the anchovy fillets. Process for 1 minute, then add resulting mixture to homemade mayonnaise. You should obtain a rather runny sauce: if too thick, add a few more spoonfuls of cooking liquid.

Slice meat and arrange slices on a serving platter. Pour sauce on top and decorate with capers and sliced olives. Refrigerate before serving.

Serves 4

Clockwise from top left: Shredded Barbecue Duck; Sliced Beef Platter with Green Sauce; Veal with Tuna Sauce

Some Festive Favorites

ROAST TURKEY WITH HERB STUFFING

11–13 lb (5–6 kg) turkey

HERB STUFFING
¾ cup (185 mL) butter, melted
2 tsp (10 mL) salt
½ tsp (2.5 mL) chopped fresh sage
½ tsp (2.5 mL) chopped fresh thyme
pepper, to taste
4 cups (1 L) soft bread cubes
¾ cup (185 mL) milk
2 stalks celery, chopped
1 small onion, chopped

BASTE
¼ cup (60 mL) orange juice
¼ cup (60 mL) butter, melted

Rinse turkey and pat dry with paper towel.

To make herb stuffing, combine all ingredients in a large bowl, adjust seasoning to taste.

Fill turkey cavity with stuffing and sew or skewer openings. Secure drumsticks under skin at tail. Place, breast side up, on rack in roasting pan. Brush turkey with baste (orange juice and butter combined), cover with aluminum foil and bake at 340°F (175°C) for 3 hours.

Remove foil, baste again and continue cooking a further 30 minutes – 1 hour to brown. Cover and allow turkey to stand 20 minutes before carving. Serve hot or cold.

Serves 12

ROAST GOOSE WITH APPLE AND PRUNE STUFFING

13 lb (6 kg) goose

APPLE AND PRUNE STUFFING
2 cups (500 mL) pitted prunes
3 large cooking apples, peeled, cored and quartered
squeeze lemon juice
freshly ground pepper, to taste

BASTE
¼ cup (60 mL) chicken stock
3 tbsp (45 mL) Calvados or brandy
¼ cup (60 mL) apple juice
freshly ground pepper

Preheat oven to 350°F (180°C). Rinse goose, remove oil sacs from tail, pat dry and prick back with skewer.

To prepare Apple and Prune Stuffing, combine all ingredients in a bowl, adjust seasoning to taste.

Fill cavity with stuffing and secure opening with skewers. Place, breast side down, on rack in roasting pan. Brush goose with baste (stock, calvados, apple juice and pepper combined), and cover with aluminum foil.

Bake for 3 hours, draining away excess fat from pan twice during cooking. Turn goose breast side up and baste with remaining mixture. Roast uncovered further 30 minutes – 1 hour. Cover and allow to stand 20 minutes before carving. Serve hot or cold.

Serves 12

BOILED FRUIT CAKE

1 cup (250 mL) water
1 cup (250 mL) brown sugar
½ lb (225 g) butter
1½ cups (375 mL) raisins, chopped
3 cups (750 mL) golden raisins
1⅔ cups (415 mL) currants
1 cup (250 mL) glacé cherries, chopped
⅓ cup (85 mL) candied mixed peel
⅓ cup (85 mL) glacé pineapple, chopped
½ tsp (2.5 mL) cinnamon
½ tsp (2.5 mL) nutmeg
½ tsp (2.5 mL) ginger
½ tsp (2.5 mL) allspice
1 tsp (5 mL) baking soda
3 eggs
3 cups (750 mL) all-purpose flour
4 tsp (20 mL) baking powder
¼ cup (60 mL) rum or dry sherry

Preheat oven to 350°F (180°C).

In large saucepan place water, brown sugar, butter, all the fruits, spices and baking soda. Cook over low heat to melt butter and blend ingredients. Allow to cool. Sift flour together with baking powder. Add flour and eggs to fruit mixture and mix evenly.

Place mixture in double-lined 8 inch (20 cm) square cake tin. (Use buttered brown paper, cutting paper 2 inches (5 cm) taller than tin.) Bake for 1½–2 hours.

Insert wooden skewer to test whether cake is cooked. When done, carefully turn out on cake rack and remove paper from base and sides. Drizzle rum over warm cake. Allow to cool completely. Wrap in wax paper and aluminum foil to store.

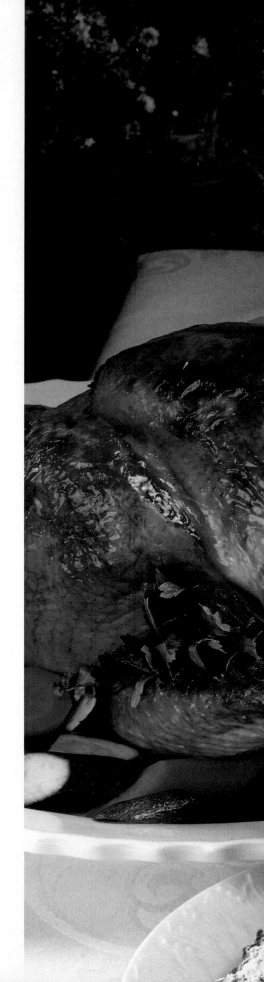

Clockwise from left: Roast Turkey with Herb Stuffing; Baked Mustard Ham; Christmas Pudding in a Cloth; Boiled Fruit Cake; Mincemeat Delight

PORK ROAST WITH CHERRY SAUCE

7–9 lb (3–4 kg) pork loin
3 tbsp (45 mL) vegetable oil
1 tbsp (15 mL) coarse salt
6 cloves garlic
12 small bay leaves

CHERRY SAUCE
½ cup (125 mL) pitted cherries
¼ cup (60 mL) corn syrup
3 tbsp (45 mL) vinegar
salt and pepper, to taste
pinch nutmeg
pinch cinnamon
pinch ground cloves

Deeply score rind of pork into ½ inch (1 cm) diamonds. Place pork loin, skin side down, in a pan and pour in 2 cups (500 mL) boiling water. Bake at 400°F (200°C) for 15 minutes. Remove pan and drain off liquid, reserving it for basting.

Add oil to pan. Rub pork skin with salt. Insert cloves and bay leaves in score marks. Roast pork, skin side up at 375°F (190°C) for 3–3½ hours. Baste with drained liquid every 30 minutes. When cooked, remove from pan, cover and allow to stand for 20 minutes before carving.

In saucepan, combine sauce ingredients, bring to boil and cook for 3 minutes until heated through.

Carve pork and serve sliced on platter with Cherry Sauce.

Serves 12

BAKED MUSTARD HAM

7–9 lb (3–4 kg) cured leg of ham
1 bay leaf
6 peppercorns
3 tbsp (45 mL) sherry
5 tbsp (75 mL) coarse-grain mustard
1 tbsp (15 mL) apricot jam

Place ham in large pot and cover with water. Add bay leaf, peppercorns and sherry. Cover with lid and bring to boil. Reduce heat and simmer for 2 hours, then allow meat to cool in liquid and drain.

Combine mustard and apricot jam. Spread over surface of ham. Place ham on rack in baking pan and cover with aluminum foil. Bake in oven at 350°F (180°C) for 1 hour. Remove foil and continue baking 45 minutes. Remove from oven and allow to cool. Serve thinly sliced.

Serves 10

Gran's Traditional Christmas Cake with candied fruit topping

GRAN'S TRADITIONAL CHRISTMAS CAKE

1 lb (450 g) butter
2 cups (500 mL) brown sugar
10 eggs
1 cup (250 mL) glacé cherries, chopped
½ cup (125 mL) mixed candied peel
3 cups (750 mL) golden raisins
3½ cups (875 mL) currants
1½ cups (375 mL) raisins, chopped
2 tsp (10 mL) ground allspice
¼ cup (60 mL) rum
1 tsp (5 mL) vanilla
¼ cup (60 mL) milk
5 cups (1.25 L) all-purpose flour
2 tsp (10 mL) baking powder

ALMOND PASTE
1 cup (250 mL) ground almonds
⅓ cup (85 mL) icing sugar
¼ cup (60 mL) fine sugar
1 egg white

ICING
2 egg whites
5 cups (1.25 L) icing sugar
1 tsp (5 mL) glycerine
2 tsp (10 mL) lemon juice
food coloring (optional)

Preheat oven to 325°F (160°C). Cream butter and sugar until smooth. Add eggs one at a time and beat mixture for 5 minutes. Add fruits, allspice, rum, vanilla and milk. Lastly add flour sifted together with baking powder and blend.

Spoon mixture into a 9 inch (22 cm) round or square cake tin double-lined with buttered brown paper. Carefully bang tin twice on counter to release air pockets from cake mix. Bake for 5–5½ hours. Insert wooden skewer to test if cake is cooked.

Stand on cake rack and cool cake in tin ½–1 hour before inverting onto cake rack to cool. Leave lining paper on cake. When cold, wrap in wax paper and aluminum foil to store. Decorate cake with icing or candied fruit.

Almond paste Blend together ground almonds and both sugars in a bowl. Stir in egg white and knead mixture to a smooth, thick paste. Dust a board with a little icing sugar and roll paste out to form a circle to fit top of cake.

Icing Beat egg whites until frothy. Add sugar gradually, beating after each addition. Add glycerine and lemon juice and beat for several minutes.

CHRISTMAS PUDDING IN A CLOTH

1½ cups (375 mL) raisins, chopped
½ cup (125 mL) blanched almonds, chopped
½ cup (125 mL) pitted dates, chopped
⅓ cup (85 mL) glacé cherries, chopped
⅓ cup (85 mL) mixed candied peel
1½ cups (375 mL) golden raisins
1⅔ cups (415 mL) currants
1 small apple, peeled and grated
½ cup (125 mL) rum or brandy
½ lb (225 g) butter
1 cup (250 mL) brown sugar
4 eggs

1 cup (250 mL) all-purpose flour
pinch salt
1 tbsp (15 mL) ground allspice
½ tsp (2.5 mL) baking soda
2½ cups (625 mL) soft white bread-crumbs
custard, brandy butter or cream, to serve

Combine chopped raisins, almonds, dates and cherries in a large bowl. Add mixed peel, golden raisins, currants and apple. Pour over rum, cover and allow to stand overnight.

Cream butter and sugar. Add eggs, beating well. Sift flour, salt, allspice and baking soda. Add breadcrumbs to flour mixture. Fold flour, butter and fruit mix-tures together. Dip pudding cloth in boiling water. Squeeze out excess moisture and lay cloth flat. Sift plenty of flour over three-quarters of cloth and rub in well – this forms a seal which prevents water seeping into pudding during cooking. Spoon mixture onto center of cloth and bring up sides of material. Secure well with string.

Bring approximately 2 quarts (2 L) water to boil. Lower pudding into water. Cover and boil pudding 4 hours, adding hot water as necessary. Remove pudding, drain and hang for 1 day. Reheat by boiling 2 hours. Remove from cloth. Serve with custard, brandy butter or cream.

Serves 12

1 Sift flour over damp pudding cloth

2 Rub in flour well to form a seal

3 Spoon pudding mixture into center
5 Bring up sides of cloth around pudding

4 Form a pudding shape with mixture
6 Secure well with string

1 Grate half the dough into the pan

2 Spread mincemeat evenly over pastry base

3 Grate remaining dough on top to cover mincemeat

MINCEMEAT DELIGHT

PASTRY
2⅓ cups (585 mL) all-purpose flour
1 tsp (5 mL) cinnamon
salt, to taste
¾ cup (185 mL) butter
½ cup (125 mL) granulated sugar
1 egg, lightly beaten

MINCEMEAT
1½ cups (375 mL) mixed dried fruit
2 cups (500 mL) canned crushed
   pineapple and juice
1 cooking apple, peeled, cored and
   grated
1 cup (250 mL) brown sugar
1 tsp (5 mL) nutmeg
1 tbsp (15 mL) cornstarch *blended
   with*
1 tbsp (15 mL) pineapple juice

Sift flour, cinnamon and salt into a bowl.
Work in butter until mixture resembles
breadcrumbs. Stir in sugar and egg to
form dough. Knead lightly then wrap in
plastic and refrigerate 1 hour. Grate half
the dough over base of 12 x 8 inch (30 x
20 cm) pan. Press down lightly and evenly with the back of a spoon. Set aside.
Preheat oven to 350°F (180°C).

   Mincemeat Place mixed fruit, pineapple and juice, apple, sugar and nutmeg in
saucepan. Add cornstarch paste and simmer until thickened. Cool slightly. Spread
mincemeat over pastry base. Grate
remaining dough over top to completely
cover mincemeat. Bake 35–40 minutes
or until golden brown. Cool on wire rack.
Cut into bars.

Makes 12–16 servings

Brunches and Lunches

Whether you are gathering together a few close friends or a crowd, brunches and lunches are a great way to entertain – indoors or out.

Here we include recipes for just about any midday menu imaginable, from light and luscious meals to barbecue specials, party-time pies plus breads and salads and the sweetest treats imaginable for dessert.

Light and Luscious

RICE SALAD WITH SHRIMP AND MUSSELS

1 cup (250 mL) rice
1 lb (450 g) freshly cooked jumbo shrimp
2 lbs (1 kg) mussels
½ cup (125 mL) dry white wine
2 lemons
½ cup (125 mL) olive oil
pepper, to taste
1 small bunch parsley, finely chopped
3 anchovy fillets, chopped

Brush mussels under running water to free shells of grit. Discard any open ones. Put them in a wide pan with wine and bring to a boil. Lift them out as soon as they open. Shell approximately half of them, reserving the other half for decoration. Peel the shrimp.

Boil rice in salted water, drain it and run some cold water through it to separate grains. Season it with juice of half a lemon, oil, plenty of pepper, parsley and anchovy fillets. Add salt if necessary.

Just before serving, stir shelled mussels and shrimp into rice, reserving some for decoration. Arrange rice in a glass bowl and decorate it with reserved shrimp, mussels in shells and lemon slices. Serve very cold.

Serves 4

Clockwise from left: Barbecue Fillet of Beef with Horseradish Cream; Mushroom Quiche; Shrimp with Creamy Satay Sauce

PAELLA

¼ cup (60 mL) olive oil
2 lbs (1 kg) chicken fillets, cut in chunks
2 onions, chopped
2 cloves garlic, crushed
¼ lb (110 g) ground pork
2 tomatoes, peeled and chopped
2 cups (500 mL) frozen peas
1⅓ cups (335 mL) canned artichoke hearts, drained and cut up
2 tsp (10 mL) paprika
1½ cups (375 mL) rice
2 tsp (10 mL) salt
4 cups (1 L) chicken stock
1 pinch saffron threads, soaked in ⅛ cup (30 mL) boiling water
1 lb (450 g) uncooked shrimp, peeled and deveined
12 mussels, scrubbed
12 black olives

Heat oil in a deep frying pan. Cook chicken, onion and garlic until brown. Add pork and brown quickly. Add tomatoes, peas, artichokes, paprika and rice. Cook, stirring, until rice is well coated with oil. Add salt, stock and saffron and cook for 15 minutes until rice is almost tender. Add shrimp and mussels and continue cooking until shrimp turn pink and mussels open. Garnish with olives.

Note: If preparing in advance, do not add shrimp and mussels until just before serving as they may toughen.

Serves 8

SEAFOOD PLATTER WITH TWO SPICY SAUCES

BEER BATTER
3 cups (750 mL) all-purpose flour
pinch salt
2 eggs, separated
2 cups (500 mL) beer
1 cup (250 mL) milk
4 tbsp (60 mL) butter, melted
oil, for deep-frying

SEAFOOD PLATTER
3 lbs (1.5 kg) fish fillets
½ lb (225 g) squid rings
1 lb (450 g) uncooked shrimp, shelled
 and deveined
½ lb (225 g) scallops
lemon twists *and* parsley, to garnish

MANGO SEAFOOD SAUCE
1 small mango, peeled, seeded and
 sliced
1 cup (250 mL) sour cream
¼ cup (60 mL) mayonnaise
2 tsp (10 mL) finely grated onion
1 tbsp (15 mL) finely chopped fresh
 coriander

LEMON MAYONNAISE
1 cup (250 mL) mayonnaise
3 tbsp (45 mL) lemon juice
1 tbsp (15 mL) finely chopped parsley
1 tsp (5 mL) finely chopped capers
freshly ground pepper

Sift flour and salt into a bowl. Make a well in the center and add egg yolks. Stir in a little of the surrounding flour. Combine beer, milk and melted butter. Gradually add beer mixture to flour, beating until smooth, then strain. Allow mixture to stand for at least 30 minutes. Whisk egg whites until stiff and fold into batter. Use at once.

Check fish fillets for bones. Heat oil for deep-frying. Dip a few pieces of the seafood at a time into the batter. Cook 6 pieces of seafood at a time until golden brown and cooked through. Drain on paper towels and serve garnished with lemon twists and parsley.

To make Mango Seafood Sauce, place mango in a food processor and purée or press through a sieve using the back of a wooden spoon. Combine with remaining ingredients and beat until smooth. Taste and adjust seasonings if desired. Serve immediately in a gravy boat.

To make Lemon Mayonnaise, combine all ingredients in a small bowl and mix until thoroughly blended. Taste and adjust seasonings if desired. Serve in a gravy boat.

Serves 10

ALMOND FRIED CHICKEN WITH SPICED GINGER SAUCE

4½ lbs (2 kg) chicken pieces
⅔ cup (165 mL) grated Parmesan
 cheese
⅓ cup (85 mL) dry breadcrumbs
¼ cup (60 mL) ground almonds
salt and pepper, to taste
2 eggs
1 tbsp (15 mL) milk
⅓ cup (85 mL) all-purpose flour
oil, for frying

SPICED GINGER SAUCE
1 tbsp (15 mL) finely grated fresh
 ginger
1 tsp (5 mL) whole allspice
1 tsp (5 mL) whole peppercorns
½ tsp (2.5 mL) mustard seed
½ tsp (2.5 mL) whole cloves
⅔ cup (165 mL) dry white wine
¼ cup (60 mL) white wine vinegar
3 tbsp (45 mL) soy sauce

Remove skin from chicken pieces. Pat dry with paper towels. Combine Parmesan, breadcrumbs, almonds, salt and pepper. Set aside. Blend together eggs and milk. Dip chicken pieces in flour then egg mixture then almond mixture. Heat oil in frying pan. Fry chicken pieces in oil, turning to brown all sides. Fry gently another 10 minutes. Drain on paper towels and serve hot or cold.

To make Spiced Ginger Sauce, combine ginger and spices in a mortar and pestle and crush lightly. If you do not have a mortar and pestle, place on a sheet of aluminum foil, fold the foil over and crush with a rolling pin. Combine white wine, vinegar and soy sauce in a small saucepan. Add spices and gently heat until boiling. Boil for 8 minutes then strain. Serve sauce in a shallow bowl suitable for dipping.

Serves 6

Left to right: Almond Fried Chicken with Spiced Ginger Sauce; Seafood Platter with Two Spicy Sauces

CHICKEN AND CHEESE SALAD WITH FRENCH DRESSING

3 cups (750 mL) torn chicory lettuce
½ head iceberg lettuce, torn
3 hard-boiled eggs, peeled and sliced
½ cup (125 mL) sliced radishes
2 tomatoes, peeled, chilled and
   quartered
1 cup (250 mL) cooked chicken strips
1 cup (250 mL) Swiss cheese strips
¼ cup (60 mL) thinly sliced ham
¼ cup (60 mL) thinly sliced tongue
¼ cup (60 mL) thinly sliced salami
½ cup (125 mL) French Dressing
   (see page 72)
anchovy fillets, to garnish

Combine chicory, iceberg, egg and radish slices. Halve mixture. Place half lettuce mixture in row on square platter. Place tomato wedges next to lettuce mixture in row. Combine chicken and cheese strips and arrange in a row alongside tomatoes. Put rest of lettuce mixture beside chicken and cheese. Complete salad platter with combined mixture of ham, tongue and salami. Coat each row lightly with salad dressing and garnish with anchovy fillets.

Serves 6

SALMON MOUSSE

1 cup (250 mL) loosely packed fresh
   dill sprigs
1 cup (250 mL) mayonnaise
2 cups (500 mL) low-fat yogurt
1 tbsp (15 mL) gelatine
1 tbsp (15 mL) lemon juice
2 slices onion
½ tsp (2.5 mL) paprika
1 lb (450 g) canned salmon
freshly ground pepper, to taste
dash Tabasco sauce
1 cucumber, peeled and sliced,
   to garnish

Chop dill and place two-thirds in a small bowl with ½ cup (125 mL) mayonnaise and 1 cup (250 mL) yogurt. Chill to serve as garnish with cucumber slices when mousse is ready.

Add gelatine, lemon juice, onion and ½ cup (125 mL) boiling water to remaining dill. Stir to dissolve gelatine. Add remaining mayonnaise and yogurt with all remaining ingredients except cucumber and stir again.

Rinse mold in cold water but do not dry. Pour in mixture and chill overnight. Serve with cucumber slice garnish and dill mayonnaise.

Serves 6–8

TURKEY AND ROQUEFORT SALAD WITH CRANBERRY DRESSING

1 cup (250 mL) shredded lettuce
3 cups (750 mL) diced cooked turkey
1 cup (250 mL) diced celery
½ cup (125 mL) seedless grapes
½ cup (125 mL) toasted pecans, chopped
1½ oz (45 g) Roquefort cheese,
   crumbled
CRANBERRY DRESSING
1 cup (250 mL) canned cranberry sauce
¼ cup (60 mL) dark soy sauce
1 small clove garlic, crushed
3 tbsp (45 mL) lemon juice
3 tbsp (45 mL) sherry
1 tbsp (15 mL) vegetable oil

Combine lettuce, turkey, celery, grapes and pecans. Pile mixture into shallow serving dish. Crumble Roquefort cheese over top of salad.

To make Cranberry Dressing, combine all ingredients in a small saucepan and heat until well blended. Serve warm in a gravy boat.

Serves 6

Turkey and Roquefort Salad with Cranberry Dressing

MARINATED LAMB SALAD

1¾ lbs (800 g) roast lamb, trimmed of
   fat and cut in strips
½ cup (125 mL) olive oil
1 cup (250 mL) red wine vinegar
¼ cup (60 mL) honey
1½ tsp (7.5 mL) salt
pinch dry mustard
2 tsp (10 mL) dried mint
¼ tsp (1 mL) oregano
¼ tsp (1 mL) thyme
¼ tsp (1 mL) aniseed
1 cucumber, peeled and sliced
4 tomatoes, quartered
½ bunch chicory lettuce
1 cup (250 mL) pitted black olives

Combine lamb with olive oil, vinegar, honey, salt, mustard, mint leaves and herbs. Refrigerate for 1 hour.

Line serving dish with cucumber, tomato quarters and chicory. Drain lamb strips, reserving dressing. Spoon lamb strips into center of dish. Combine dressing and olives. Pour over meat and vegetables to serve.

Serves 6

Marinated Lamb Salad

Barbecue Specials

BARBECUED FISH

2 x 4 lb (2 kg) whole cleaned fish
   (porgy, snapper or mullet)
2 lemons
salt and freshly ground pepper,
   to taste
3 onions, sliced in rings
½ lb (225 g) mushrooms, sliced
4 tomatoes, sliced
5 tbsp (75 mL) butter
lemon wedges, to serve

Remove scales and wipe fish with a damp cloth. Peel rind from 1 lemon, cut into julienne strips and simmer for a few minutes; drain and cool. Squeeze lemons and brush lemon juice over both fish. Season with salt and pepper. Place fish on 2 large pieces of aluminum foil, shiny side down. Spread onion rings over both fish, then cover with mushrooms and tomatoes. Season with pepper and dot butter over

fish. Drizzle over any remaining lemon juice and sprinkle with lemon rind julienne. Wrap fish in foil, folding to seal.

Cook fish over glowing coals for 25–40 minutes or until cooked when tested. Fish should flake. (Cooking time will depend on heat of fire and thickness of fish.) Serve fish with the vegetables and cooking juices. Garnish with lemon wedges.

Serves 10–12

BARBECUED FILLET OF BEEF WITH HORSERADISH CREAM SAUCE

3 lb (1.5 kg) beef fillet
4–6 slices bacon

MARINADE
1 carrot, roughly chopped
1 onion, roughly chopped
1 cup (250 mL) port wine
½ cup (125 mL) vegetable oil
few peppercorns
1 tsp (5 mL) whole allspice
1 clove garlic, crushed

HORSERADISH CREAM SAUCE
1 cup (250 mL) whipping cream,
   whipped and chilled
1 tbsp (15 mL) prepared horseradish
   or horseradish cream
1 green onion, finely chopped
1 tbsp (15 mL) finely chopped parsley

Trim fillet of excess fat and all sinew. Place on a board and wrap bacon around in a spiral fashion. Secure with toothpicks. Combine all marinade ingredients and place with fillet in a strong plastic bag. Secure bag opening and ensure fillet is covered with marinade. Refrigerate overnight, turning bag from time to time. Remove fillet from marinade and pat dry with paper towels.

Cook fillet over moderately hot barbecue coals for about 10–12 minutes for a medium rare steak or 15–20 minutes for a medium steak. Test with a skewer, then remove from barbecue and stand meat for 10 minutes before carving. Carve thin slices across the grain. Arrange on a platter and serve with Horseradish Cream Sauce.

To make sauce, combine all ingredients, stir until blended and serve in a bowl.

Serves 10

Left to right above: Shrimp with Creamy Satay Sauce and Barbecued Fillet of Beef with Horseradish Cream; below: Tandoori Chicken; Shrimp with Creamy Satay Sauce; Barbecued Fish

HONEYED LAMB KEBABS

3 lbs (1.5 kg) lean lamb, trimmed
    and diced
¼ cup (60 mL) white wine
3 tbsp (45 mL) hoisin sauce
3 tbsp (45 mL) sherry
3 tbsp (45 mL) honey
1 clove garlic, crushed
salt and freshly ground pepper,
    to taste
1 large onion, cut into wedges

Marinate lamb in combined wine, hoisin sauce, sherry, honey and garlic. Season, cover and refrigerate overnight. Drain and reserve marinade to use as a baste during cooking.

Soak satay sticks or wooden skewers in boiling water to cover for 10 minutes. Drain and thread lamb dice onto satay sticks interspersed with wedges of onion. Cook kebabs under a preheated hot broiler or over a barbecue, basting occasionally with marinade. Turn to cook and brown each side.

Serves 6–8

MINTY LAMB BURGERS

5–6 lbs (2.5–3 kg) boned leg of lamb
2 onions, finely chopped
1–2 cloves garlic, crushed
3 tbsp (45 mL) chopped mint
1 tsp (5 mL) paprika
salt and freshly ground pepper,
    to taste
3 eggs, beaten

TO SERVE
½ lb (225 g) butter
3–4 tbsp (45–60 mL) chopped mint

Trim all skin and visible fat off lamb, then cut into pieces. Mince, using a food processor or meat grinder. Avoid processing the lamb too finely.

Place ground meat in a bowl with onions, garlic, mint, paprika, salt, pepper and eggs and mix well. Cover and refrigerate.

Beat butter until soft. Add mint and beat again. Taste for mint flavor and add freshly ground pepper. Spoon butter onto a sheet of foil and roll into a log shape. Refrigerate until serving time.

Divide lamb mixture into 20 parts. With wet hands, shape each into a burger shape. Cook over glowing coals for 5–10 minutes until done. Serve burgers topped with a thin slice of mint butter.

Serves 10–12

Minty Lamb Burgers

TANDOORI CHICKEN

16–20 chicken pieces
2 large onions, grated
3 cloves garlic, crushed
juice of 3 lemons
1 tsp (5 mL) salt
1½ cups (375 mL) plain yogurt
2 tbsp (30 mL) ground coriander
2 tsp (10 mL) turmeric
2 tsp (10 mL) ground chili pepper
2 tsp (10 mL) black mustard seeds,
    ground
red food coloring (optional)

Remove skin from chicken and prick flesh several times with a skewer. Mix onions, garlic, lemon juice and salt. Rub all over the chicken and leave for 30 minutes.

Combine yogurt, spices and food coloring, if used. Pour yogurt mixture over chicken, stirring to coat all pieces. Cover and marinate for at least 12 hours in the refrigerator. Cook chicken over glowing coals for 20–30 minutes or until cooked.

Serves 10–12

SHRIMP WITH CREAMY SATAY SAUCE

½ cup (125 mL) peanut butter
1 clove garlic, crushed
3 tbsp (45 mL) light soy sauce
finely grated rind and juice of 1 lemon
1 tsp (5 mL) dried shrimp paste
1–2 red chili peppers, seeded and
    finely chopped
½ cup (125 mL) cream
2 lbs (1 kg) uncooked jumbo shrimp,
    shelled, deveined, with tails on

Combine all ingredients except cream and shrimp in a small saucepan. Stir over gentle heat until well blended. Remove from heat and stir in cream.

Soak 20 bamboo skewers in boiling water for 10 minutes (this will prevent them burning when barbecuing). Thread shrimp onto skewers and cook over hot coals, basting frequently with sauce. Serve with any remaining sauce.

Serves 10

The Party-time Pie Shop

CHICKEN AND MUSHROOM PIE

3 lbs (1.5 kg) chicken
3 tbsp (45 mL) dry sherry
6 black peppercorns
2 tsp (10 mL) chopped fresh herbs
¼ tsp (1 mL) sage
½ tsp (2.5 mL) salt
¼ cup (60 mL) sliced leek
½ cup (125 mL) chopped onion
1 clove garlic, crushed
¼ cup (60 mL) butter
½ lb (225 g) fresh mushrooms, sliced
freshly ground pepper
12 sheets filo pastry
6 tbsp (90 mL) butter, melted
1 tbsp (15 mL) sesame seeds

Clean and rinse chicken. Place in large saucepan with sherry, peppercorns, herbs and salt. Cover with cold water and bring to boil. Simmer for 45 minutes. Allow to cool in liquid then drain, discarding stock. Remove skin and bones from chicken and discard. Cut up chicken meat and set aside.

Sauté leek, onion and garlic in butter until transparent. Add mushrooms and pepper and cook 2 minutes. Add mushroom mixture to chicken meat, stirring to blend. Place chicken mixture in 8 inch (20 cm) pie plate.

Cut pastry sheets in half to cover top of pie plate. Place between 2 dry tea towels and cover with a barely damp tea towel to keep pastry moist. Layer pastry over filling, brushing every second sheet with butter. Roughly tuck pastry around edge of dish. Brush with butter and sprinkle with sesame seeds.

Bake on top rack at 400°F (200°C) for 45 minutes or until golden brown. Serve hot.

Serves 6–8

MUSHROOM QUICHE

¾ lb (340 g) ready-made frozen
    shortcrust pastry, thawed
3 tbsp (45 mL) butter
1 large onion, finely chopped
1 clove garlic, crushed
¾ lb (340 g) button mushrooms, sliced
juice of ½ lemon
4 eggs
1½ cups (375 mL) cream
salt and freshly ground pepper, to
    taste

Halve pastry, roll out and line 2 x 9 inch (22 cm) quiche pans. Preheat oven to 400°F (200°C). Place wax paper over pastry and weigh down with rice grains. Bake blind for 10 minutes. Remove paper and rice and bake pastry a further 5 minutes, then set aside.

Heat butter and sauté onion and garlic for 5 minutes. Add mushrooms and sauté 3–5 minutes. Remove from heat and add lemon juice.

Beat eggs, add cream and beat again. Season with salt and pepper. Spoon mushrooms into pastry bases then pour on cream mixture. Bake quiches for 15 minutes. Reduce temperature to 350°F (180°C) and bake a further 20–25 minutes until cooked when tested. Allow to cool then serve sliced.

Serves 12

BACON AND ASPARAGUS QUICHE

PASTRY

1¾ cups (440 mL) all-purpose flour
salt, to taste
4 tbsp (60 mL) butter
1 egg yolk, beaten
cold water

FILLING

2 slices bacon, chopped
2 green onions, chopped
1½ tbsp (20 mL) butter
5 eggs
6 tbsp (90 mL) cream
½ cup (125 mL) grated Cheddar cheese
½ oz (14 g) blue cheese, crumbled
1 medium-sized tomato, sliced
8–10 canned asparagus spears

Preheat oven to 425°F (220°C).

Sift flour and salt into a bowl and work in butter until mixture resembles breadcrumbs.

Stir in egg yolk and sufficient water to form soft dough. Knead dough on lightly floured board. Roll out to fit 9 inch (22 cm) quiche pan, trimming to fit. Prick base of pastry and bake blind for 10 minutes.

Sauté bacon, green onions and butter for 2 minutes. Beat eggs and cream together, then strain. Fold in grated cheeses and bacon mixture.

Place tomato slices on pastry base, top with asparagus spears and pour egg mixture over. Reduce oven temperature to 375°F (190°C) and bake for 45 minutes or until set and browned on top. Serve hot or cold.

Serves 6–8

VEGETARIAN PIE

PASTRY
1½ cups (375 mL) all-purpose flour
¼ tsp (1 mL) baking powder
pinch salt
2 tsp (10 mL) curry powder
¼ lb (110 g) butter
3 tbsp (45 mL) chopped onion

FILLING
½ lb (225 g) spinach, washed and chopped
1 onion, chopped
1½ tbsp (20 mL) butter
1 cup (250 mL) canned beans of your choice, drained
1 cup (250 mL) canned creamed corn
1 tbsp (15 mL) chopped parsley
1 tsp (5 mL) salt
1 tbsp (15 mL) tomato catsup
dash Tabasco sauce
1⅓ lb (600 g) cottage cheese
1 egg
paprika, to taste

Preheat oven to 400°F (200°C). Sift flour, baking powder, salt and curry powder into a bowl. Rub in butter until mixture resembles breadcrumbs. Add onion and enough water to form dough. Knead dough lightly on floured board. Roll out to fit 9 inch (22 cm) quiche pan. Trim edges and prick with fork. Bake blind for 10 minutes.

Sauté spinach and onion in butter over low heat for 2 minutes. Drain excess liquid. Layer spinach, onion, beans, creamed corn and parsley on base. Combine salt, catsup, Tabasco, cottage cheese and egg. Pour over vegetable filling and sprinkle with paprika. Return to oven and bake for 30 minutes. Serve hot or cold.

Serves 6

Clockwise from top: Chicken and Mushroom Pie; Bacon and Asparagus Quiche; Mushroom Quiche

Salads on the side

GREEN SALAD WITH DIJON MUSTARD DRESSING

3 cups (750 mL) torn spinach
½ head lettuce, torn
4 stalks celery, chopped
½ green pepper, diced
1 cucumber, rinsed and sliced
3 tbsp (45 mL) chopped chives
6 green olives, pitted and sliced
1 avocado, pitted, peeled and sliced

DIJON MUSTARD DRESSING
1 tbsp (15 mL) vinegar
3 tbsp (45 mL) vegetable oil
1 tsp (5 mL) Dijon mustard
freshly ground pepper

Wash and drain spinach and lettuce and combine with celery and green pepper. Place row of cucumber slices around edge of salad dish. Sprinkle chives over.

To make dressing, combine all ingredients in a screw-top jar and shake well.

Toss spinach mixture with dressing, pile into center of serving dish and garnish salad with olives and avocado slices.

Serves 6

MARINATED CUCUMBER AND ONION

2 medium-sized cucumbers, peeled and sliced
2 tsp (10 mL) salt
¼ cup (60 mL) white vinegar
¼ cup (60 mL) water
½ tsp (2.5 mL) sugar
¼ tsp (1 mL) paprika
¼ tsp (1 mL) pepper
½ clove garlic, crushed
6 green onions, sliced, to serve

Place cucumber slices in a shallow bowl. Combine salt, vinegar, water, sugar, paprika, pepper and garlic and pour over cucumber slices, tossing lightly to coat. Cover and chill in refrigerator for 3 hours. Garnish with sliced green onions to serve.

Serves 6

AVOCADO AND LETTUCE SALAD WITH MUSTARD SEED DRESSING

1 head lettuce
2 avocados, peeled, sliced and sprinkled with
juice of ½ lemon
1 small cucumber, peeled and sliced
6 green onions, trimmed
alfalfa sprouts

MUSTARD SEED DRESSING
3 tbsp (45 mL) plain yogurt
1 tbsp (15 mL) vegetable oil
2 tsp (10 mL) mustard seeds
1 tsp (5 mL) grated fresh ginger

Wash and dry lettuce. Refrigerate 30 minutes until crisp then tear into bite-sized pieces. Place in salad bowl. Top with avocado slices. Add cucumber and garnish with green onions and alfalfa sprouts.

To make dressing, combine all ingredients, mixing until smooth. Just before serving pour over salad and toss.

Serves 8–10

CITRUS AND MANGO SALAD WITH CREAM DRESSING

1 head lettuce
3 oranges, peeled and white pith removed
3 stalks celery, cut into 3 inch (8 cm) pieces
16 oz (450 g) can mango slices, drained
1 cucumber, scored and sliced
6 green onions, finely sliced

CREAM DRESSING
¼ cup (60 mL) mayonnaise
½ cup (125 mL) cream
salt and freshly ground pepper
3 tbsp (45 mL) chopped parsley
1 tsp (5 mL) Dijon mustard
1 tbsp (15 mL) orange juice
2 tsp (10 mL) lemon juice

Wash lettuce and arrange leaves on a serving plate. Segment the oranges. To make celery curls, slice the celery lengthwise leaving one end uncut. Drop celery into iced water until it curls.

Arrange mango slices, orange segments, celery curls and cucumber on lettuce leaves. Garnish with green onions and refrigerate until ready to serve.

To make dressing, mix all ingredients well, stand 15–20 minutes before using and serve separately.

Serves 6–8

EXOTIC FLOWER SALAD

1 large mango
1 tbsp (15 mL) lemon juice
1 tbsp (15 mL) salad oil
salt, to taste
¼ lb (110 g) mushrooms, thinly sliced
freshly ground pepper
1 large head lettuce
1 tbsp (15 mL) chopped herbs
3 tbsp (45 mL) pine nuts, toasted
2 oz (60 g) snowpeas, topped, tailed and blanched
1 endive, separated into leaves
1 quantity Creamy Vinaigrette Dressing (see recipe)

Peel the mango and cut a thick slice from each side of pit and set aside for the salad. Cut remaining flesh from pit and purée. Add lemon juice, oil and salt. Combine purée with the mushrooms and pepper, and toss lightly.

Arrange lettuce leaves on plates in a flower shape with the mushrooms in middle. Sprinkle over the chopped herbs and nuts, arrange mango slices, snowpeas and endive on the plate. Drizzle Creamy Vinaigrette Dressing on top and serve.

Serves 6

RED CABBAGE NUT SLAW WITH TAHINI ORANGE DRESSING

3 cups (750 mL) shredded red cabbage
1 cup (250 mL) shredded green cabbage
½ cup (125 mL) whole toasted blanched almonds

BASE DRESSING
3 tbsp (45 mL) cream
1 tbsp (15 mL) tarragon vinegar
1 tsp (5 mL) prepared mustard
¼ tsp (1 mL) garlic salt

TAHINI ORANGE DRESSING
3 tbsp (45 mL) tahini
3 tbsp (45 mL) water
juice and finely grated rind of 1 orange

Combine red and green cabbage, wash, drain and chill in refrigerator. Combine base dressing ingredients in a screw-top jar and shake well. Toss cabbage with dressing and ¼ cup (60 mL) almonds. Pile into salad bowl and top with remaining almonds. To serve, spoon over Tahini Orange Dressing.

Serves 6

Clockwise from top: Avocado and Lettuce Salad with Mustard Seed Dressing; Red Cabbage Nut Slaw with Tahini Orange Dressing; Green Salad with Dijon Mustard Dressing

The Bread Board

Combine ingredients of the filling of your choice. Slice bread and spread slices with filling. Put the loaf back together again and wrap in aluminum foil. Bake at 400°F (200°C) for 10 minutes, open the foil wrapping and bake a further 5-10 minutes until loaf is crisp and cheese is hot. Serve immediately in bread basket.
Note: Bread loaves can be filled, wrapped in foil and frozen ready for baking.

PATAFLA

1 baguette or other long French loaf
6 tomatoes, peeled and chopped
1 onion, finely chopped
6 green onions, finely chopped
2 green peppers, seeded and chopped
1 red pepper, seeded and chopped
1½ cups (375 mL) black olives, pitted and chopped
¼ cup (60 mL) capers
3 gherkins, chopped
freshly ground pepper, to taste
¼ cup (60 mL) olive oil

Halve the loaf lengthwise and scoop out the inside. Place crumbs in a bowl with vegetables, olives, capers and gherkins, stir mixture well, add pepper then stir in oil.
   Divide tomato mixture between 2 bread halves. Reassemble and wrap firmly in foil. Refrigerate overnight. Cut into thin slices to serve.

Serves 10–12

HOT-FILLED LOAVES

1 long French loaf

FRENCH ONION BREAD
8 oz (225 g) package cream cheese
1 envelope French onion soup mix

CHEESE AND CHIVE BREAD
¼ cup (60 mL) butter
8 oz (225 g) package cream cheese
3 tbsp (45 mL) chopped parsley
3 tbsp (45 mL) chopped chives
3 tbsp (45 mL) chopped fresh herbs
freshly ground pepper

GARLIC AND HERB BREAD
3 cloves garlic, crushed
¼ lb (110 g) butter
3 tbsp (45 mL) chopped parsley
pinch mixed herbs

MUSSEL BREAD
4 oz (110 g) can smoked mussels, drained
8 oz (225 g) package cream cheese
1 tbsp (15 mL) chopped parsley

HAM AND BLUE CHEESE BREAD
¼ lb (110 g) butter
1 tbsp (15 mL) chopped parsley
2 oz (60 g) ham, finely chopped
1 oz (28 g) blue cheese

WHOLEWHEAT NUT BREAD

1 tbsp (15 mL) dry yeast
2 tsp (10 mL) sugar
3 tbsp (45 mL) warm water
2¼ cups (560 mL) whole-wheat flour
1 cup (250 mL) all-purpose flour
2 tsp (10 mL) salt
¼ cup (60 mL) wheat germ
¼ cup (60 mL) crushed pecan nuts
2 tbsp (30 mL) butter, melted
1¼–1¾ cups (310-440 mL) lukewarm milk
1 egg, beaten

Combine yeast, sugar and warm water. Leave in a warm place for a few minutes to bubble. Sift flours and salt in bowl, stir in yeast mixture, wheat germ, pecans, butter and ¾ cup (185 mL) milk. Sprinkle surface with flour. Cover with plastic wrap and stand in warm place for 15 minutes. Combine enough of remaining milk with flour mixture to form dough. Place on floured board and knead for 10 minutes. Place in greased bowl. Cover with plastic wrap. Stand 30–40 minutes in warm place until mixture doubles in quantity. Punch dough down. Divide in half and knead each into log shape.
   Place in 2 greased loaf pans. Cover with plastic wrap. Allow dough to rise to top of tin. Preheat oven to 425°F (220°C). Glaze with beaten egg and bake for 15 minutes; reduce heat to 400°F (200°C) and continue cooking 30–40 minutes. Cool on cake rack.

Makes 2 loaves

Clockwise from bottom left: Hot-Filled Loaves; Patafla; Savory Scone Roll

Left to right: Damper; Fruit and Tea Damper

DAMPER

4 cups (1 L) self-rising flour
1 tsp (5 mL) salt
2 tbsp (30 mL) butter
1 cup (250 mL) milk
½ cup (125 mL) water

Sift together flour and salt into a large mixing bowl. Using fingertips gently rub in butter till mixture resembles fine breadcrumbs. Make a well in the center and gradually add combined milk and water mixing with knife to form a soft, slightly sticky dough. Turn dough onto a lightly floured board and knead to form a smooth round shape.

Lightly grease a baking sheet or pie plate. Place dough on pan and bake at 400°F (200°C) for 25 minutes, then reduce heat to 350°F (180°C) and bake a further 15–20 minutes until the loaf sounds hollow when tapped. Serve sliced with butter or jam.

Makes 1 loaf

FRUIT AND TEA DAMPER

½ cup (125 mL) chopped dried apricots
½ cup (125 mL) chopped raisins
¾ cup (180 mL) dried dates, pitted and chopped
finely grated rind of 1 orange
2 cups (500 mL) warm tea
¼ cup (60 mL) butter, softened
1 tsp (5 mL) ground allspice
3 tbsp (45 mL) sugar
1 quantity Damper dough *(see recipe)*

Combine fruits in a small bowl, cover with tea and set aside for 30 minutes to soak. Drain very well then combine with butter, allspice and sugar. Pat Damper dough out to form a circle about 12 inches (30 cm) in diameter. Place fruit in the center. Fold edges of circle towards center (the circle should now be a square) and pinch edges together to encase filling.

Carefully place Fruit Damper on a greased baking sheet and brush lightly with a little beaten egg. Bake at 400°F (200°C) for 25 minutes, then reduce heat to 350°F (180°C) and bake a further 15–20 minutes, or until well risen. Cool slightly before serving, otherwise the filling will be too hot.

Makes 1 loaf

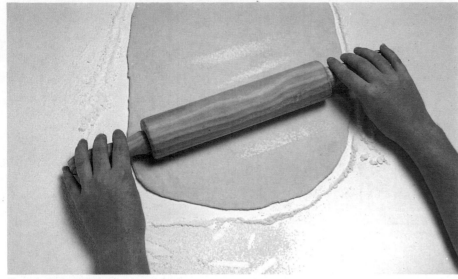

Savory Scone Roll
1 Roll pastry out flat

SAVORY SCONE ROLL

3 cups (750 mL) self-rising flour
pinch cayenne pepper
1 tsp (5 mL) salt
¼ cup (60 mL) butter
1 cup (250 mL) milk

FILLING
2 slices bacon, diced and cooked
1 cup (250 mL) grated aged Cheddar
1 tbsp (15 mL) coarse grain mustard
½ tsp (2.5 mL) paprika
1 egg, beaten, to glaze

Sift flour, cayenne pepper and salt in a large mixing bowl. Rub butter into flour until mixture resembles breadcrumbs. Make a well in the center and gradually add milk, mixing with a knife to form a soft dough. Turn dough out onto a lightly floured board and knead.

Roll out dough to form a rectangle, 12 x 10 inches (30 x 25 cm). Combine filling ingredients and sprinkle over dough leaving a 1 inch (2.5 cm) border of dough around the edges. Starting at the longest edge, roll up jelly roll fashion to enclose filling. Place seam side down on baking pan. Lightly brush with beaten egg.

Bake at 400°F (200°C) for approximately 20 minutes or until roll is well risen and golden brown, then serve hot.

Serves 6

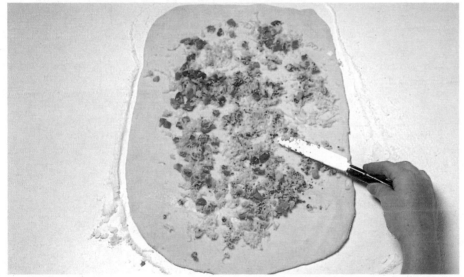

2 Spread filling evenly

3 Roll up pastry

43

The Sweetest Treats Imaginable

BRANDY ORANGE SAVARIN

2 cups (500 mL) all-purpose flour
¼ tsp (1 mL) salt
1 tbsp (15 mL) dry yeast
1 tbsp (15 mL) sugar
⅔ cup (165 mL) warm milk
2 eggs, beaten
¼ lb (110 g) softened butter
¼ cup (60 mL) glacé cherries
2 glacé pineapple rings, cut into
  eighths

SYRUP
⅔ cup (165 mL) water
⅓ cup (85 mL) orange juice
1 cup (250 mL) sugar
½ inch (1 cm) piece vanilla bean
¼ cup (60 mL) brandy

GLAZE
½ cup (125 mL) sweet orange
  marmalade
1 tbsp (15 mL) water
1 tbsp (15 mL) orange liqueur
  (eg Curaçao or Cointreau)

Sift flour and salt together in a bowl. Combine yeast, sugar and warm milk. Make well in flour. Add yeast mixture. Sprinkle over a little flour. Cover with plastic wrap. Allow to rise in a warm place for 15 minutes.

Add eggs and softened butter and mix to a smooth elastic dough. Cover mixture with plastic wrap and again leave in a warm place to double in bulk – about 30 minutes.

Place mixture into well-greased 9 inch (22 cm) ring mold or cake pan. Allow to stand, covered with plastic wrap, until mixture rises to top of tin. Bake at 400°F (200°C) for 20 minutes.

Combine ingredients for syrup in saucepan. Stir over heat until sugar dissolves. Bring to boil, boil for 10 minutes, then strain. While Savarin is hot, pour over hot syrup. Allow Savarin to stand 30 minutes until syrup is absorbed. Turn onto serving plate.

To make glaze, combine marmalade, water and orange liqueur in saucepan. Heat for 5 minutes. Glaze Savarin with three-quarters of mixture. Decorate with glacé cherries and pineapple pieces. Drizzle over remaining glaze. Serve sliced with whipped cream.

Serves 8

MOCHA CHEESECAKE

CRUST
1½ cups (375 mL) chocolate wafer
  crumbs
1 cup (250 mL) walnuts, crushed
¼ lb (110 g) butter, melted

FILLING
1¾ cups (440 mL) whipping cream,
  whipped
3 eggs, separated
8 oz (225 g) package cream cheese
¼ cup (60 mL) sugar
1 tbsp (15 mL) instant coffee combined
  with 1 tbsp (15 mL) hot water
¼ cup (60 mL) chocolate liqueur
2 tsp (10 mL) gelatine
¼ cup (60 mL) hot water, extra

GARNISH
⅔ cup (165 mL) whipping cream,
  whipped
chocolate curls
glacé cherries

Combine wafer crumbs, walnuts and melted butter. Press crumb mix into base of 9 inch (22 cm) spring-form cake pan. Bake at 375°F (190°C) for 10 minutes then chill.

Whip cream. Cream egg yolks together with cream cheese. Blend in sugar, coffee and hot water and chocolate liqueur. Dissolve gelatine in extra hot water over low heat. Whisk egg whites until stiff. Combine egg whites, whipped cream, cream cheese mixture and gelatine. Blend evenly. Pour cheesecake mixture into tin.

Chill overnight in refrigerator. Remove outside of spring-form pan. Whip extra cream. Pipe rosettes of whipped cream onto top of cheesecake. Decorate with chocolate curls and glacé cherries. Return to refrigerator until ready to serve.

Serves 6–8

FUDGE CAKE

¾ cup (185 mL) butter
¾ cup (185 mL) sugar
1 tbsp (15 mL) honey
3 eggs
2 cups (500 mL) self-rising flour
4 tsp (20 mL) baking powder
⅔ cup (165 mL) milk
½ tsp (2.5 mL) almond extract

CREAM FILLING
¼ lb (110 g) butter
1½ cups (375 mL) icing sugar
juice of ½ lemon

FUDGE ICING
¼ lb (110 g) butter
1 tbsp (15 mL) honey
3 tbsp (45 mL) milk
2 cups (500 mL) icing sugar
flaked almonds and chocolate curls,
  to garnish

Preheat oven to 400°F (200°C). Cream butter and sugar until light and fluffy. Add honey and eggs, beating well. Sift flour and baking powder and add to butter mixture alternately with milk and almond extract.

Divide mixture between 3 8-inch (20 cm) greased and lined cake pans. Bake for 18–20 minutes or until cooked when tested. Remove from pans to cake rack and allow to cool.

To make Cream Filling, beat butter and icing sugar together with lemon juice. Sandwich cake layers together with cream mixture.

To make Fudge Icing, combine butter, honey and milk in saucepan. Gently heat until butter melts, then heat until nearly boiling. Remove from heat and sift in icing sugar, beating until icing thickens. Spread icing over top of cake and allow to drizzle down the sides. Cool and decorate with almonds and chocolate curls.

Clockwise from left: Mocha Cheesecake; Meringue Baskets; Brandy Orange Savarin

CHOCOLATE LIQUEUR ROLL

¼ lb (110 g) baking chocolate
3 tbsp (45 mL) strong black coffee
4 eggs, separated
¾ cup (185 mL) sugar
3 tbsp (45 mL) cocoa, sifted
½ cup (125 mL) whipping cream, whipped
1 tbsp (15 mL) kirsch liqueur
extra ¼ cup (60 mL) whipping cream, whipped
4 strawberries, cut into fans

Melt chocolate in top of double boiler with the coffee. Beat egg yolks and sugar until thick. Whisk egg whites until stiff. Fold melted chocolate into egg yolks. Fold in egg whites. Spoon mixture into greased and lined jelly roll pan. Bake at 412°F (210°C) for 10 minutes. Turn off oven. Leave cake mixture for 15 minutes in oven. Remove from oven, leave cake in pan, cover with damp tea towel till cool. Turn out onto a sheet of wax paper dusted with cocoa. Spread with whipped cream flavored with Kirsch. Roll up and chill. Decorate with whipped cream rosettes and strawberry fans.

Serves 8–10

PECAN NUT MERINGUES

3 egg whites
pinch cream of tartar
1 cup (250 mL) granulated sugar
⅔ cup (165 mL) chopped pecans
20 crushed saltine crackers
1 tsp (5 mL) vanilla
1 tsp (5 mL) cornstarch
extra pecans
½ cup (125 mL) whipping cream, whipped

Whisk egg whites with cream of tartar until stiff. Gradually add sugar. Beat until stiff. Fold in chopped pecans, crushed crackers and vanilla.

Lightly dust baking sheet with cornstarch. Drop mixture by tablespoonfuls 3 inches (7.5 cm) apart on baking sheet, spread out to 2 inch (5 cm) circles. Bake at 300°F (150°C) for 30 minutes. Transfer to serving plate. Allow to cool and decorate with nuts and whipped cream.

Serves 6–8

45

PARTY COCKTAIL TRIFLE

1 oz (28 g) package red jelly powder
2 cups (500 mL) boiling water
1 large jam-filled jelly roll
¼ cup (60 mL) sherry
2⅓ cups (585 mL) milk
2 eggs
3 tbsp (45 mL) cornstarch
vanilla extract
3 tbsp (45 mL) sugar
1¼ cups (310 mL) whipping cream, whipped
3 tbsp (45 mL) shredded coconut, toasted

Combine jelly powder and boiling water until dissolved. Pour into shallow baking pan. Allow to set in refrigerator then cut up roughly. Slice Swiss roll into ½ inch (1 cm) slices. Line base and sides of glass serving dish with cake slices. Sprinkle sherry over cake slices.

In large saucepan combine milk, eggs, cornstarch, vanilla and sugar and whisk till fluffy. Bring to boil, whisking, until thickened. Allow to cool slightly. Pour over cake slices. Chill overnight. Top with jelly and pipe with whipped cream to decorate. Sprinkle with toasted coconut before serving.

Serves 6–8

BLACK FOREST CRÊPE CAKE

CRÊPE MIXTURE
pinch salt
2 cups (500 mL) all-purpose flour
2 eggs
2⅓ cups (585 mL) milk
1½ tbsp (20 mL) butter

FILLING
16 oz (440 g) can pitted black cherries
¼ cup (60 mL) orange-flavored liqueur
3 tbsp (45 mL) sugar
3 tbsp (45 mL) cornstarch

GARNISH
1 cup (250 mL) whipping cream, whipped
¼ cup (60 mL) almond flakes, toasted

Sift salt and flour together; blend in eggs and milk to form a smooth batter.

Grease crêpe pan with butter. Pour 1 tbsp (15 mL) crêpe mix into hot pan, turn pan to cover base thinly with mixture. Cook one side only until dry on surface. Continue until 15–20 crêpes have been made. Layer crêpes between paper towels and allow to cool.

Place cherries with their liquid, liqueur, sugar and cornstarch in saucepan. Bring to a boil, stirring. Allow to thicken and then cool. Mold crêpes together with cherry filling, spreading filling between each layer, to make a dome shape.

Whip cream. Coat outside of crêpes with cream. Decorate cake with toasted almonds. Refrigerate until serving time. Serve sliced.
Note: Keeps 1–2 days in refrigerator.

Serves 10–12

MERINGUE BASKETS

2 egg whites
½ cup (125 mL) granulated sugar
¼ tsp (1 mL) cream of tartar

Whisk egg whites until stiff. Add sugar and cream of tartar, beating well for 20 minutes. Fit piping bag with large rosette tube. Fill with egg white mixture and pipe meringue in small 4 inch (10 cm) rounds forming a basket shape on lightly oiled baking sheet.

Bake at 225°F (110°C) until crisp but still white. Baking time can vary from 2–4 hours. Allow to cool in oven. Fill baskets with whipped cream and fruit and serve.

Makes 8

VARIATIONS
CHOCOLATE MERINGUE BASKETS
Add 2 tsp (10 mL) sieved cocoa

COFFEE MERINGUE BASKETS
Add 2 tsp (10 mL) instant coffee

Left to right: Meringue Baskets; Party Cocktail Trifle; Mocha Cheesecake

Black Forest Crêpe Cake

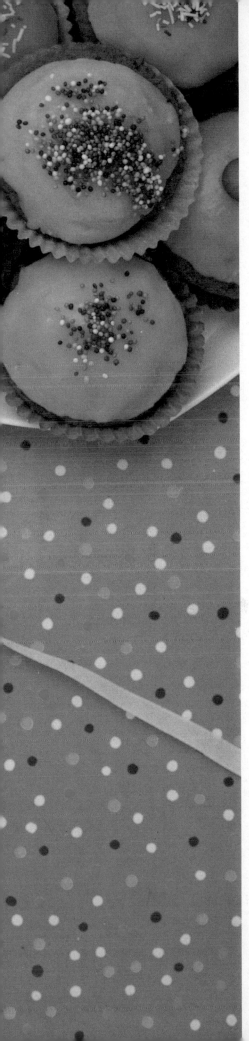

Children's Birthday Parties

Sugar and spice and all things nice: that's what children's birthday parties are made of. The excitement which builds over the weeks is almost unmanageable by The Day. This chapter of savory and sweet recipes brings together ideas for parties for toddlers through to the more sophisticated palates of young teenagers.

Savory Beginnings

TRAFFIC LIGHTS

24 slices brown bread
4 tbsp (60 mL) butter
4 processed cheese slices
4 small tomatoes, sliced
6 lettuce leaves, shredded
salt and pepper, to taste
¼ cup (60 mL) shredded carrot

Spread bread slices lightly with butter. Cut crusts from bread. Using a round ½ inch (1 cm) cookie cutter, press 2 rows of 3 holes each into 12 of the bread slices. Cut each slice of processed cheese into thirds. Cover the uncut 12 slices of bread with tomato, cheese and lettuce side by side in traffic light colors, then top with salt, pepper and carrot. Top with cut-out slices of bread. Cut each sandwich in half to make traffic lights.

Makes 24

RIBBON SANDWICHES

4 slices white bread
4 slices brown bread
softened butter
3–6 different sandwich fillings
    (see below)

Remove crusts from bread. Thinly butter bread. Spread 1 of the fillings on a slice of white bread. Top with slice of brown bread. Spread with second filling. Continue layering bread, using alternate slices of white and brown bread and spreading with filling. Cut sandwich in half, then each half into 4, making ribbon layer sandwiches.

Makes 8

PINWHEELS

1 loaf unsliced white bread
softened butter
3–6 different sandwich fillings
    (see below)

Remove crusts from loaf of bread. Cut bread in half crosswise. Carefully slice each half into 8 slices lengthwise. Thinly butter each slice and spread evenly with filling. Roll up each slice lengthwise and secure each roll with toothpick. Continue with remaining bread and filling.

Makes 8

SANDWICH FILLINGS

☆ Finely chopped meat or seafood with mayonnaise
☆ Mashed salmon
☆ Cream cheese mixed with finely chopped dried fruits/walnuts/chives/celery/finely grated lemon or carrot
☆ Finely mashed egg with mayonnaise
☆ Chopped lettuce and ham
☆ Cheese spread or herbed processed cheese
☆ Mashed sardines
☆ Chicken and celery mixed with mayonnaise
☆ Peanut butter and golden raisins
☆ Peanut butter and honey
☆ Peanut butter and finely shredded lettuce
☆ Mashed banana, lemon juice and shredded coconut

Children's party cakes

HOT TUNA BREAD

1 French bread stick
7 oz (200 g) can tuna, drained
1 small onion, chopped
1 stick celery, chopped
3 tbsp (45 mL) mayonnaise
1 tbsp (15 mL) chopped parsley
1 tsp (5 mL) lemon juice
pepper, to taste
3 slices processed cheese

Preheat oven to 350°F (180°C). Halve bread lengthwise and scoop out crust. Mix together tuna, onion, celery, mayonnaise, parsley, lemon juice and pepper. Spoon tuna mixture into bread case.

Halve cheese slices diagonally. Layer cheese over top of tuna. Cover with top of bread stick. Wrap in foil and bake for 25 minutes. Five minutes before serving, open foil so that cheese will melt and bread will become crusty. Serve in slices.

Serves 6

PIZZA

2 cups (500 mL) all-purpose flour
pinch salt
1 tbsp (15 mL) dry yeast
½ tsp (2.5 mL) sugar
⅔ cup (165 mL) warm milk
2½ tbsp (40 mL) olive oil

TOPPING
4 tomatoes, sliced
2 onions, sliced and separated into rings
½ lb (225 g) salami, sliced
1 tsp (5 mL) mixed herbs
½ cup (125 mL) grated mozzarella cheese
1 tbsp (15 mL) chopped parsley
3 tbsp (45 mL) olive oil

OPTIONAL EXTRAS
¼ cup (60 mL) chopped olives
½ cup (125 mL) sliced mushrooms
½ cup (125 mL) cooked peeled shrimp

Sift flour and salt into a bowl. Combine yeast, sugar, warm milk and olive oil. Cover and leave in a warm place for 5 minutes or until bubbly.

Make a well in center of flour, pour in milk mixture. Sprinkle with flour, cover with plastic wrap and leave in a warm place for 15 minutes until yeast mixture bubbles again.

Work mixture to form dough. Knead dough on floured board for 10 minutes or until smooth and elastic. Halve and roll out each piece to an 8 inch (20 cm) circle; for smaller pizzas, roll each piece of dough into five 3 inch (8 cm) rounds. Place on greased baking sheets.

Divide topping ingredients between pizzas. Place layer of tomato slices on dough, add onions rings, salami, mixed herbs and mozzarella cheese. Top with parsley and sprinkle with olive oil. Allow pizzas to stand for 15 minutes. Preheat oven to 400°F (200°C). Bake for 40 minutes and serve hot.
Note: Sprinkle any of the extras over the salami layer. Pizza crusts, wrapped well in plastic, may be frozen for up to 6 months.

Makes two 8 inch (20 cm) pizzas or ten 3 inch (8 cm) pizzas

CHINESE SPRING ROLLS

1 tbsp (15 mL) vegetable oil
1 onion, finely chopped
¼ lb (110 g) lean ham, diced
¼ lb (110 g) bean sprouts
1 tsp (5 mL) soy sauce
oil, for deep-frying
8 spring roll wrappers

Heat oil in wok and stir-fry onions until transparent. Add ham and bean sprouts, stir-fry gently for 1½ minutes. Stir soy sauce through mixture. Allow to cool.

Spoon 3 tbsp (45 mL) ham and onion filling on to each spring roll wrapper, fold over at ends and roll up, pressing edges in firmly. Stand for 15 minutes.

Heat oil in wok. Deep-fry spring rolls until golden. Serve hot with commercial plum sauce.

Serves 4

BACON-WRAPPED BEEF AND APPLE BURGERS

1¾ lbs (800 g) ground lean beef
⅓ cup (85 mL) breadcrumbs
¼ cup (60 mL) finely chopped onion
1½ tsp (7.5 mL) Worcestershire sauce
pepper, to taste
2 apples, grated
6 slices bacon

Combine beef, breadcrumbs, onion, Worcestershire sauce, pepper and apple in a bowl. Form mixture into 6 patties. Wrap a bacon slice round each burger, securing with toothpick. Grill burgers for 10 minutes, turning once to brown each side. Serve on hamburger bun with salad and sauce.

Serves 6

SAY CHEESE PIES

2 cups (500 mL) all-purpose flour
pinch cayenne pepper
6 tbsp (90 mL) butter
1 cup (250 mL) grated sharp cheddar
3–4 tbsp (45–60 mL) ice water
milk, to glaze

FILLING
1 large onion, sliced
2 tbsp (30 mL) butter
2 hard-boiled eggs, peeled and chopped
½ lb (225 g) cheddar cheese, diced
1 tbsp (15 mL) chopped parsley
½ tsp (2.5 mL) nutmeg
pepper, to taste

Sift flour and cayenne into a bowl. Work in butter with pastry cutter till mixture resembles fine breadcrumbs. Add cheese and water to form dough.

Knead lightly on floured board. Roll out dough to ¼ inch (0.5 cm) thickness. Cut into 16 rounds to fit tart tins. Press 8 rounds into base of tart tins. Prick base lightly. Set aside. Preheat oven to 425°F (220°C).

Sauté onion in butter until transparent, drain. Combine onion with remaining filling ingredients and divide filling between pastry-lined tins. Dampen edges of pastry, cover with remaining pastry rounds. Seal edges together. Make small hole in center of top of each pie. Brush with milk. Bake for 30 minutes then remove from tins to rack. Serve hot or cold.

Makes 8

Pizzas (above) and Pinwheel Sandwiches (below)

SESAME DRUMSTICKS

8 chicken drumsticks
¼ cup (60 mL) all-purpose flour
  with salt and pepper
1 egg, beaten
¼ cup (60 mL) sesame seeds
¼ cup (60 mL) toasted breadcrumbs
¼ cup (60 mL) butter, melted

Wipe drumsticks, dip in seasoned flour, then beaten egg and coat in combined sesame seeds and breadcrumbs.

Place drumsticks on greased baking pan and bake at 350°F (180°C) for 30 minutes. Brush drumsticks with butter. Continue cooking a further 15–20 minutes or until golden brown. Serve hot or cold.

Makes 8

SAVORY EGG BOATS

6 hard-boiled eggs
7 oz (200 g) can tuna, drained
½ cup (125 mL) finely chopped celery
¼ cup (60 mL) mayonnaise
pepper, to taste
¼ tsp (1 mL) dry mustard
3 slices toasted bread
finely chopped parsley, to garnish

Peel and halve eggs lengthwise. Remove yolks from whites and mash yolks finely. Combine mashed yolks with tuna, celery, mayonnaise, pepper and mustard and pile into egg white halves. Cut crusts off bread. Cut each piece of toast into 4 triangles. Insert 1 triangle on top of each stuffed egg boat to resemble a sail. Garnish with chopped parsley. Refrigerate until serving time.

Makes 12

BUSH BABY SALAD

2 cups (500 mL) alfalfa sprouts
2 celery stalks
½ cup (125 mL) raisins
¼ lb (110 g) cherry tomatoes, halved
4 carrots, peeled and cut into
  matchsticks
1 cup (250 mL) corn kernels

Spread alfalfa sprouts over a large serving plate. Cut celery into 2 inch (5 cm) lengths and arrange attractively on the alfalfa with the remaining ingredients.

Serves 6

SAUSAGE AND BACON BRAID

10 oz (280 g) package frozen ready-
  made puff pastry, thawed
1 egg, beaten
1 tbsp (15 mL) sesame seeds

FILLING
¾ lb (340 g) ground pork
⅓ lb (150 g) bacon, chopped
1 onion, chopped
1 tbsp (15 mL) chopped parsley
salt and pepper, to taste
¼ tsp (1 mL) mixed herbs

Roll out pastry to 10 inch (25 cm) square on a lightly floured surface. Combine filling ingredients and place along center of pastry. Cut pastry on each side of filling into diagonal strips ½ inch (1 cm) wide. Brush with beaten egg.

Place strips from each side alternately over the sausage mixture to form a braid. Place braid onto lightly greased baking sheet, glaze with egg, sprinkle with sesame seeds and bake at 400°F (200°C) for 30–40 minutes or until cooked. Serve hot.

Serves 6

TUNA AND NOODLE BAKE

¾ cup (180 mL) macaroni, cooked
7 oz (200 g) can tuna, drained
⅓ cup (85 mL) mayonnaise
½ cup (125 mL) chopped celery
salt and pepper, to taste
10 oz (300 g) can condensed cream
  of celery soup
⅓ cup (85 mL) milk
1 cup (250 mL) grated aged cheddar
¼ cup (60 mL) breadcrumbs
1 tbsp (15 mL) chopped parsley,
  to garnish

Combine cooked drained macaroni, tuna, mayonnaise, celery, salt and pepper. Blend together soup and milk over heat, stirring until heated through, but do not boil. Add half the cheese, stir until melted. Fold soup mixture into macaroni and noodle mixture. Place into 2 quart (2 L) casserole dish. Sprinkle with remaining cheese and breadcrumbs. Bake at 350°F (180°C) for 20 minutes. When cooked, sprinkle with parsley to serve.

Serves 6

MEATBALL BOATS

1 lb (450 g) ground beef
1 cup (250 mL) grated aged cheddar
3 tbsp (45 mL) catsup
pepper, to taste
½ cup (125 mL) desiccated coconut
15 cheese slices
30 thin sticks cucumber

Combine meat, cheese, catsup and pepper. Shape mixture into about 30 meatballs. Toss in coconut until well coated. Place on greased baking pan and bake at 400°F (200°C) for 15 minutes.

Cut each cheese slice into 2 triangles. Place 1 cheese slice and 1 cucumber stick together. Secure through top and bottom with toothpick to form the mast and sail. Attach to the meatball. Serve meatballs hot or cold.

Makes 30

SPICY CHICKEN PIECES

1 cup (250 mL) soy sauce
½ cup (125 mL) vegetable oil
1 tbsp (15 mL) grated fresh ginger
½ cup (125 mL) chicken stock
2 tsp (10 mL) Chinese five-spice
  powder
3 tbsp (45 mL) honey
3 lbs (1.5 kg) chicken pieces

Combine first 6 ingredients in a small saucepan and heat until simmering. Remove from heat. Pat chicken pieces dry with paper towels and place in a large dish. Pour over soy sauce mixture, cover and refrigerate for at least 6 hours.

Lift chicken pieces from marinade, arrange in baking dish and bake at 350°F (180°C) for 30 minutes, basting occasionally with remaining marinade. To test if chicken is cooked, pierce flesh with a skewer. The juices should run clear without any signs of pink. Serve hot or cold. *Note:* If serving chicken at a barbecue, cook over moderately hot coals turning frequently.

Serves 10

Clockwise from top left: Sausage and Bacon Braid; Bush Baby Salad; Sesame Drumsticks; Savory Egg Boats

COCKTAIL BANANA KEBABS

6 cocktail wieners
2 bananas, peeled
3 slices bacon
6 x 1 inch (2.5 cm) pieces pineapple
6 button mushrooms

Thread cocktail wieners onto skewers. Cut each banana into thirds. Add piece banana to skewer. Cut slices of bacon in half. Roll each half and secure onto skewer. Finish with piece of pineapple then mushroom.

Place under preheated broiler and cook until all sides are browned. Serve hot.

Serves 6

KIWI AND NUT SALAD

1 head lettuce
4 kiwis, peeled and sliced
2 oranges, peeled and segmented
4 radishes, thinly sliced
1 cup (250 mL) button mushrooms, thinly sliced
small cucumber, thinly sliced
1 stick celery, thinly sliced
⅓ cup (85 mL) cashew nuts
¼ cup (60 mL) French Dressing (see recipe)
shredded orange peel, to garnish

Tear lettuce into pieces. Mix all ingredients together in salad bowl and toss with dressing. Alternatively, dressing may be served separately. Garnish with fine shreds of orange peel.

Serves 4–6

WATERMELON SALAD

½ watermelon
1–2 cantaloupes
3 cups (750 ml) cooked rice
16 oz (450 g) can whole kernel corn, drained
1 lb (450 g) red grapes, peeled and seeded
1 lb (450 g) green grapes, peeled and seeded
mint or basil leaves, to garnish

Remove watermelon seeds. Scoop all flesh out of melons using a melon baller. Combine ingredients and pile into watermelon shell. Cover with foil or plastic wrap and chill. Serve garnished with mint or basil leaves. Vinaigrette Dressing (see recipe) can be poured over salad if desired.

Serves 6–8

Sweet Treats

TOFFEE APPLES

10 red apples
TOFFEE
½ lb (225 g) butter
1 cup (250 mL) sugar
¼ cup (60 mL) water
¼ tsp (1 mL) salt
1 tsp (5 mL) vanilla

Remove stalks from apples and push a wooden skewer into each one.

Place toffee ingredients in saucepan and heat until sugar dissolves, stirring occasionally. Bring to boil. Boil rapidly, without stirring, until the toffee reaches 280°F (140°C) on a candy thermometer or until a spoonful of mixture, when dropped in cold water, separates into threads which are hard but not brittle. Carefully dip apples into toffee one at a time. Cover apple completely. Plunge into ice water for 5 seconds. Stand on well-oiled wax paper until set.

Makes 10

ALPHABET COOKIES

¼ lb (110 g) butter
½ cup (125 mL) granulated sugar
2 cups (500 mL) all-purpose flour
¼ tsp (1 mL) baking powder
2 egg yolks
1 tsp (5 mL) vanilla extract
1 tsp (5 mL) grated lemon rind
pinch salt
candy sprinkles
chocolate sprinkles
¼ cup (60 mL) chopped glacé cherries

ICING
1 cup (250 mL) icing sugar
3–4 tbsp (45–60 mL) lemon juice

Preheat oven to 400°F (200°C). Cream together butter and sugar. Fold in flour, baking powder, egg yolks, vanilla extract, lemon rind and salt to form a stiff dough. Wrap dough in plastic wrap and refrigerate 1 hour.

Roll out dough to 12 inch (30 cm) square. Cut into 26 x ½ inch (1 cm) blocks. Roll each into sausage shape about ½ inch (1 cm) in diameter, shape into the 26 alphabet letters and flatten slightly. Place on greased baking sheet and bake for 8–10 minutes. Allow to cool on tray 2 minutes before removing to cake rack.

Stir icing sugar with lemon juice to make a thick icing. Ice letters while still warm. Decorate with candy sprinkles, chocolate sprinkles or glacé cherries. Allow to cool and set.

Makes 26

POPCORN BALLS

20 cups (5 L) popped corn
1½ cups (375 mL) molasses
¼ cup (60 mL) water
½ cup (125 mL) sugar
1 tbsp (15 mL) vinegar
½ tsp (2.5 mL) salt
⅓ cup (85 mL) butter
1 tbsp (15 mL) vanilla

OPTIONAL ADDITIONS
1 cup (250 mL) shredded coconut
1 cup (250 mL) raisins
1 cup (250 mL) salted peanuts
1 cup (250 mL) puffed wheat

Put the popcorn in a very large, warm bowl. Stir in any optional additions at this point.

In saucepan combine molasses, water, sugar, vinegar and salt. Cook over medium heat, stirring occasionally, until mixture heats to 275°F (135°C) on a candy thermometer or a small amount dropped into ice water separates into hard but not brittle threads.

Remove from heat and add ⅓ cup (85 mL) butter and vanilla. Gradually pour hot syrup into the center of the popped corn. Quickly stir corn and syrup to coat.

With buttered hands, gather and press corn into firm balls. Push wooden skewer into ball. Allow to cool. Wrap each ball in a square piece of cellophane, drawing the paper around the ball and twisting on top.

Makes 15

Clockwise from top: Emerald Smoothie; Cupcakes; Toffee Apples; Popcorn; Alphabet Cookies

SIMPLE SPONGE LAYER CAKE

Delicious as a simple sponge cake or decorated as a birthday cake, this is a very useful basic recipe.

BATTER
¼ lb (110 g) butter
½ cup (125 mL) granulated sugar
2 eggs
1 cup (250 mL) self-rising flour

DECORATION
4 tbsp (60 mL) jam
icing sugar

Preheat oven to 340°F (175°C). Cream butter and sugar together until soft. Whisk eggs, beat into sugar mixture. Fold in flour. Spoon mixture into 2 greased and lined 6 inch (15 cm) sponge cake pans. Bake for 20 minutes. Remove cakes from tins and cool on cake rack.

Spread jam onto first cake and sandwich it to second. Sprinkle top with icing sugar, or frost and decorate as a birthday cake.

SERVING SUGGESTIONS

Try decorating your cake with some of the following: flowers, small toys, marzipan miniature fruits, smarties, jelly beans, or other candies, candy sprinkles, glacé fruits, silver dragees, whipped cream, sliced fresh fruit, candles and anything else that appeals to your imagination. Little athletes may like a cricket cake (shown) or a baseball cake: use green icing for the grass, coconut for the diamond, chocolate squares for bases, and plastic figurines to represent players. Some girls may like heart-shaped cakes with plenty of fancy icing decorations. Try using different shaped tins – there is plenty of variety available.

JELLY CUPCAKES

1 quantity Simple Sponge Layer Cake batter *(see recipe)*
2 x 1 oz (28 g) packages raspberry-flavored jelly powder
2 cups (500 mL) boiling water
2 cups (500 mL) shredded coconut
1¼ cups (310 mL) whipping cream, whipped

Make Sponge batter according to directions. Lightly grease 18 cupcake tins. Place 2–3 tbsp (30–45 mL) of cake mixture into each cupcake tin and bake in the top half of the oven at 350°F (180°C) for 15–20 minutes or until well risen and golden brown. Turn out onto a cake rack to cool.

Dissolve jelly powder in boiling water and pour into a heatproof dish deep enough to cover a cupcake. Place in refrigerator and allow to partially set. The jelly should resemble the consistency of egg white. Sprinkle coconut on a large sheet of wax paper. Dip each cupcake in jelly then roll in coconut to coat. If a thicker coating is desired, repeat process.

Place jelly cupcakes in a single layer on a tray and refrigerate until set. One or 2 hours before serving, cut a little off the top of each cupcake. Place a small spoonful of cream on each cupcake and replace their tops before serving.

Makes approximately 18

Cricket Cake (see Simple Sponge Layer Cake) with Jelly Cupcakes

THE GINGERBREAD LOG CABIN

2 lbs (1 kg) thick honey
1 cup (250 mL) water
5 cups (1.25 L) rye flour
3½ cups (875 mL) whole-wheat flour
1 cup (250 mL) chopped mixed
  candied peel
1 tsp (5 mL) ground ginger
1 tsp (5 mL) cinnamon
½ tsp (2.5 mL) nutmeg
1 tsp (5 mL) baking soda

ICING
2 egg whites
3 cups (750 mL) icing sugar
1 tbsp (15 mL) lemon juice

DECORATION
glacé cherries
blanched almonds
candies
plastic toy trees and figurines

Bring honey and water to boil in a saucepan, stirring continuously. Leave to cool.

Sift flours and add mixed peel, spices and baking soda. Make well in center and add honey mixture. Blend mixture into a soft dough. Refrigerate dough wrapped in plastic wrap overnight.

Divide dough into 6 equal portions. If dough is too stiff set it in a warm place for 15 minutes until easy to handle.

To make roof, roll out 2 portions to ¼ inch (0.5 cm) thickness and 8 inches (20 cm) square. Set aside on lightly greased baking sheet and prick with a fork.

To make walls, use 3 portions of dough and roll into sausage shapes about ½ inch (1 cm) in diameter.

The 4 walls require a total of:
    28 logs 8 inches (20 cm) long
    4 logs 7½ inches (19 cm) long
    2 logs 6½ inches (17 cm) long
    2 logs 5½ inches (14 cm) long
    2 logs 5 inches (12.5 cm) long
    2 logs 4 inches (10 cm) long

To make each end wall, place on lightly greased baking sheet side by side:
    7 x 8 inch (20 cm) logs
    1 x 7½ inch (19 cm) log
    1 x 6½ inch (17 cm) log
    1 x 5½ inch (14 cm) log
    1 x 5 inch (12.5 cm) log
    1 x 4 inch (10 cm) log

To make remaining 2 walls, place on a greased baking sheet side by side:
    7 x 8 inch (20 cm) logs
    1 x 7½ inch (19 cm) log

Preheat oven to 400°F (200°C). Bake roof 12–18 minutes then cool on cake rack. Leaving a tiny ⅛ inch (2 mm) gap between each log, bake each wall 12–18

minutes. During baking, the gaps will close to form the wall. Allow to cool on rack.

From 1 wall cut out:
    1 door 1 x 2½ inches (2.5 x 6.5 cm)
    1 window 1½ x 1 inches (4 x 2.5 cm)
With remaining dough, make:
    4 logs 1 inch (2.5 cm) long and
    ¼ inch (1 cm) thick
On baking tray place 2 logs next to each other and 2 logs on top to make double layer – this forms the chimney.

Knead remaining uncooked dough. Roll into flat ¼ inch (0.5 cm) thick square 9 x 9 inch (22 x 22 cm). This will form the base of the house. Prick with fork. Place on tray with chimney logs and bake 12–18 minutes. Cool on cake rack.

Whisk egg whites and fold in icing sugar to form smooth paste. Add lemon juice.

Place house base on bread board. Using icing, join 4 walls together at corners on top of base. Allow to dry completely at each stage of construction. Join roof to house with icing.

Thin 4 tbsp (60 mL) of icing with a few drops of water. Gently drizzle icing over roof to resemble snow. Attach chimney to roof.

Divide window cut-out in half. Place each half on either side of window to resemble shutters and attach with icing. Decorate house and garden with icing, cherries, nuts, candies and figurines. Allow to set completely.

1 Make 2 walls and 2 end walls
3 Join roof to house with icing

2 Join walls
4 Drizzle icing over roof to make snow

CUPCAKE PARADE

1 quantity Simple Sponge Cake batter
   (see recipe)
GLAZE
1½ cups (375 mL) icing sugar, sifted
1 tsp (5 mL) butter
2–3 tbsp (30–45 mL) boiling water
few drops food colorings of your
   choice

Line 2 cupcake trays with paper cups and fill two-thirds full with spoonfuls of Sponge Cake batter. Bake at 350°F (180°C) for 15–20 minutes or until cupcakes are well risen and golden brown. Turn out onto a wire rack to cool before icing.

To make icing, combine icing sugar and butter in a bowl and beat; gradually add enough boiling water to mix. Add colorings, leaving 1 bowl of icing white. Ice cupcakes and decorate imaginatively: use white icing to pipe names of party guests or rosettes onto iced cupcakes; garnish with candy sprinkles, chocolate sprinkles, silver dragees, glacé cherries, jellybeans, smarties or other favorite candies. Let your imagination create a colorful variety where every cupcake is different – they look wonderful massed together on large trays or serving platters. *Note:* To achieve a smooth finish on your icing, use a round bladed knife and dip from time to time in hot water. Cupcakes without icing can be made in advance and frozen.

Makes 24

CHOCOLATE BUTTERFLY CAKES

¼ lb (110 g) butter
½ cup (125 mL) granulated sugar
2 eggs, beaten
¾ cup (185 mL) self-rising flour
¼ cup (60 mL) cocoa
1 tbsp (15 mL) warm water
chocolate sprinkles, to decorate
⅔ cup (165 mL) whipping cream,
   whipped

Preheat oven to 375°F (190°C). Cream butter and sugar till smooth. Beat in eggs. Fold in sifted flour and cocoa alternately with water. Beat mixture 2 minutes. Spoon mixture into 20 paper-lined cupcake tins. Bake for 15 minutes. Cool on a cake rack. Cut tops off cakes and halve. Spoon 1–2 tsp (10 mL) of cream on top of each cake and press in the tops to form wings. Sprinkle each butterfly with chocolate sprinkles.

Makes 20

SUPERB CHOCOLATE CAKE

2 cups (500 mL) all-purpose flour
⅔ cup (165 mL) granulated sugar
⅓ cup (85 mL) cocoa
1 tbsp (15 mL) baking powder
1 tsp (5 mL) baking soda
pinch salt
1 cup (250 mL) milk
¼ lb (110 g) butter or margarine, melted
2 eggs

Preheat oven to 375°F (190°C). Grease an 8 inch (20 cm) cake tin.

Sift dry ingredients twice in a bowl. Combine milk and butter and add to dry ingredients. Beat with an electric mixer for 2 minutes. Add eggs and beat again for 2 minutes.

Bake in a preheated oven for 50–60 minutes or until cooked when tested. Remove and cool on a cake rack. Ice with chocolate icing and decorate as desired.

ALMOND CHOCOLATE FUDGE

¾ lb (340 g) semi-sweet baking
   chocolate
10 oz (300 mL) can condensed milk
2 tsp (10 mL) vanilla
1 cup (250 mL) roasted almonds,
   chopped

Melt chocolate in top of double boiler. Blend in condensed milk, stirring until combined. Remove from heat. Add vanilla and beat until smooth. Fold in almonds. Pour mixture into greased square cake pan. Chill in refrigerator until set. When firm, cut into 1 inch (2.5 cm) squares.

Makes 40 squares.

NOUGAT WALNUT SPONGE CAKE

SPONGE CAKE
12 eggs, separated
1 cup (250 mL) sugar
3 cups (750 mL) self-rising flour
½ tsp (2.5 mL) baking soda
pinch salt

FILLING
¼ lb (110 g) nougat
¼ cup (60 mL) apricot preserve
¼ cup (60 mL) butter
¼ cup (60 mL) sugar
1 tbsp (15 mL) boiling water
1 tbsp (15 mL) milk
¼ tsp (1 mL) vanilla
1 cup (250 mL) crushed walnuts
1 small can peach slices, drained
¼ cup (60 mL) glacé cherries
¼ cup (60 mL) water
2 tsp (10 mL) sugar
2 tsp (10 mL) gelatine

Blend egg yolks and sugar together. Sift flour, baking soda and salt together. Whisk egg whites till stiff. Fold egg yolks, flour mixture and egg whites together.

Grease and line the base of a 9 or 10 inch (23–25 cm) spring-form cake pan. Place one-third of cake mix into pan. Bake at 350°F (180°C) for 10–15 minutes or until lightly browned. Remove from pan immediately. Remove paper from base, allow to cool. Repeat to make second and third layers of cake.

Place 1 layer on serving plate. Melt nougat in a double boiler and spread over cake base. Spread thin layer apricot preserve over nougat. Add second cake layer. Cream butter and sugar till smooth and sugar is dissolved. Gradually blend in boiling water. Beat 2 minutes. Fold in walnuts. Spread walnut cream over cake layer.

Add remaining cake layer. Decorate with peach slices. Place cherries, water, sugar and gelatine in saucepan. Bring to boil; boil 2 minutes. Cool slightly, spoon over top of cake and allow to set. Serve sliced.
Note: Refrigerate no more than 3 days.

Serves 12–16

RAINBOW CAKE

½ lb (225 g) butter
1 tsp (5 mL) vanilla
1 cup (250 mL) sugar
4 eggs
2½ cups (625 mL) self-rising flour
1 cup (250 mL) all-purpose flour
¾ cup (185 mL) milk
1 drop red food coloring
2 oz (60 g) chocolate, melted

FILLING
⅓ cup (85 mL) raspberry jam
1¼ cups (310 mL) whipping cream,
   whipped

VANILLA ICING
¼ lb (110 g) white chocolate
2 cups (500 mL) icing sugar
⅔ cup (165 mL) milk
½ lb (225 g) butter
1 tsp (5 mL) vanilla

Preheat oven to 400°F (200°C). Cream together butter, vanilla and sugar. Add eggs, one at a time, and beat well. Sift flours and fold in alternately with milk. Divide mixture evenly into three. Leave one third plain, color one third pink with red food coloring, and add melted chocolate to remaining third.

Spoon different colored mixtures in alternating rows into 2 greased cake pans (see step by step). Bake for 20–25 minutes. Cool on cake rack. When cold, sandwich layers together with raspberry jam and whipped cream, and ice with vanilla icing.

To make icing: Melt chocolate in top of double boiler. Blend together icing sugar, milk, butter and vanilla, fold in melted chocolate. Allow to set and decorate as desired.

Rainbow Cake

1 Divide cake mixture between three bowls

2 Leave one bowl plain and color one pink

3 Add melted chocolate to third bowl

4 Place white and pink mixtures in alternating rows using two-thirds of pan

5 Add a final row of the chocolate mixture along one side of pan

FROZEN FRUIT POPSICLES

2 cups (500 mL) strawberries, washed
½ cup (125 mL) concentrated apple juice
½ cup (125 mL) unsweetened pineapple juice

Place strawberries in a food processor or blender and blend until smooth. Add remaining ingredients and blend a further 30 seconds. Transfer mixture into a jug and pour into popsicle molds. Place in freezer and freeze for at least 6 hours.

Makes 12

ORANGE BOMBS

12 large oranges
2 quarts (2 L) vanilla ice cream
¾ cup (185 mL) orange juice concentrate, well chilled but not frozen
finely grated rind of 1 orange
few drops orange food coloring (optional)
orange leaves or blossoms, to garnish (optional)

Cut top third from each orange. Using a small knife, loosen orange flesh from just inside skin. Carefully scoop down into the oranges and remove as much flesh and membrane as possible. Reserve orange flesh for fruit juice.

Remove ice cream from freezer and allow to soften slightly. Place in large mixing bowl and, using a metal spoon, stir in remaining ingredients. If ice cream starts to soften too much, return to freezer for a few minutes.

Place orange shells on baking trays. Spoon ice cream into shells until almost full (the filling will expand when frozen). Place in freezer for 2 hours, then remove and wrap in plastic wrap. Return to freezer. Place bombs in refrigerator for 30 minutes before serving. The ice cream filling will soften slightly and the orange shells will collect a frosty 'bloom'. Serve topped with orange leaves or blossoms if in season.

Makes 12

Left to right: Frozen Fruit Popsicles and Orange Bombs

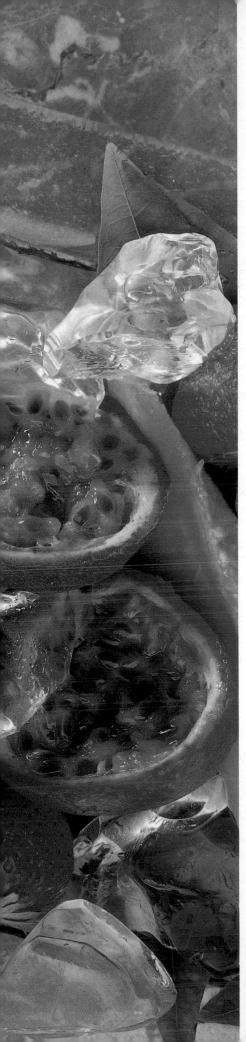

Diet Delights

These days, everyone is aware of the importance of their health and well-being. At a time when more people enjoy international cuisine, no one wants to subsist on carrot sticks and shriveled lettuce. The following recipes from around the world offer delicious, attractive and health-conscious party dishes.

Delicious Soups

CHILLED LEEK AND POTATO SOUP

4 leeks
1½ tbsp (20 mL) polyunsaturated margarine or unsalted butter
2 lbs (1 kg) potatoes, peeled and sliced
8 cups (2 L) homemade Chicken Stock *(see recipe)*
freshly ground pepper, to taste
1 cup (250 mL) low-fat yogurt
3 tbsp (45 mL) chopped chives

Remove darker green leaves from leeks. Halve leeks lengthwise almost to the root end. Wash well, separating leaves to clean. Drain, cut off root ends and slice.

Heat margarine, add leeks, cover pan and cook for 5 minutes. Add potatoes, and stock and pepper. Bring to a boil, reduce heat and simmer for 20–30 minutes until potato is tender. Set aside to cool.

Drain soup, reserving cooking liquid. Purée cooked vegetables in batches, adding reserved liquid as necessary. Combine purée and remaining cooking liquid and adjust seasoning. About 1 hour before serving, stir in yogurt. Serve soup chilled, sprinkled with chives.

Serves 10–12

CREAMY CARROT SOUP

2 tsp (10 mL) polyunsaturated oil *or* margarine
1 onion, finely chopped
1 clove garlic, crushed
2 lbs (1 kg) carrots, peeled and chopped
4 cups (1 L) Chicken Stock *(see recipe)*
freshly ground pepper, to taste
1 cup (250 mL) low-fat yogurt
1 tsp (5 mL) cornstarch
4–5 tbsp (60–75 mL) chopped parsley
3 tbsp (45 mL) chopped chives, to garnish

Heat oil in pan, add onion and garlic and sauté 5 minutes, stirring occasionally. Add carrots, chicken stock and pepper and bring to boil. Reduce heat and simmer, partially covered, for about 20 minutes until carrot is tender. Cool for a few minutes.

Purée soup, return to rinsed pan and reheat soup gently. Add some hot soup to combined yogurt and cornstarch mixture and stir well. Add yogurt mixture to soup and heat, stirring.

Just before serving, add parsley. Pour soup into a heated tureen and serve garnished with chives.

Serves 10–12

Salad Greens with Tomato Dressing and Fruit

GAZPACHO

2 lbs (1 kg) tomatoes, peeled, seeded and chopped
½ cucumber, seeded and diced
3–4 cloves garlic, finely chopped
4 green onions, thinly sliced
½ green pepper, diced
3 tbsp (45 mL) oil, olive or polyunsaturated
2–3 tbsp (30–45 mL) white wine vinegar
salt (optional)
freshly ground pepper, to taste
Tabasco sauce, to taste
¼ cup (60 mL) chopped parsley
2½ cups (625 mL) ice water

GARNISH
½ cucumber, seeded and diced
½ green pepper, diced
3 slices whole-wheat bread, diced

Combine tomatoes, cucumber, garlic, green onions, green pepper, oil and vinegar with salt, pepper, Tabasco sauce and parsley; chill well. Just before serving stir in ice water.

Serve soup in chilled bowls. Place cucumber, green pepper and bread in small bowls. Guests can help themselves to garnish as desired.

Note: 2 eggs, hard-boiled, can be chopped and offered as another garnish.

Serves 10–12

HERBED YOGURT AND CUCUMBER SOUP

4 cups (1 L) low-fat yogurt
2 cups (500 mL) Chicken Stock (see recipe)
chopped garlic, to taste
2 cucumbers
⅓ cup (85 mL) pecans, very finely chopped
2–3 tbsp (30–45 mL) oil, olive or polyunsaturated
1–3 tbsp (15–45 mL) chopped mint
1 tbsp (15 mL) chopped dill
freshly ground pepper, to taste

Place yogurt in a bowl and beat well. Stir in chicken stock and garlic and chill in refrigerator.

If cucumber has a thick or waxed skin, peel it, otherwise leave the skin on. Halve the cucumbers lengthwise and scoop out seeds. Dice cucumber flesh. Stir cucumber into yogurt mixture with remaining ingredients. Serve chilled.

Serves 10–12

CHICKEN STOCK

2 lbs (1 kg) chicken backs or carcass
water, to cover
1 onion, studded with 3 cloves
few celery leaves
1 carrot, roughly chopped
bouquet garni *(see glossary)*
½ tsp (2.5 mL) whole black peppercorns

Wash chicken, discard skin and trim off fat. Place bones in a pan with water to cover and bring to boil, skimming as necessary. Add remaining ingredients, reduce heat and simmer partially covered, for 1½–2 hours. Skim as necessary.

Strain stock and allow to cool. Chill overnight and remove any fat that has risen to the surface. Use stock as directed.

To store: Refrigerate for up to 1 week, simmering every 2–3 days. Alternatively freeze in usable quantities. 1 cup (250 mL) quantities are a useful size. It is always handy to have frozen cubes of chicken stock, so another useful method is to freeze 2 ice-cube trays of stock. Place frozen cubes into a plastic bag, seal and label.

Makes approximately 4 cups (1 L)

International Smorgasbord

MUSSELS AND SNOW PEAS

2 lbs (1 kg) mussels
½ lb (225 g) snow peas, trimmed
10–12 fresh lychees, peeled
4 slices fresh ginger, finely sliced
½ cup (125 mL) Tomato Dressing (see recipe)

Scrub mussels and pull out beard. Discard any mussels with broken or open shells. Bring 1 cup (250 mL) water to boil, add mussels, cover and steam for 3–5 minutes until they open. Discard any unopened mussels. Remove mussels from shells and place in a bowl. Cover and set aside.

Cover snow peas with boiling water and leave for 1 minute. Drain and cool with water. Add snow peas to mussels. Halve lychees and remove pits. Arrange with mussels. Sprinkle ginger over.

Pour dressing over mussel mixture and stir to coat all ingredients. Cover and chill for 30 minutes. Drain off any excess dressing. Serve on individual plates.

Serves 10–12

FISH WITH HERBED YOGURT DRESSING

16 fish fillets
few parsley stalks
few celery leaves
1 tsp (5 mL) black peppercorns
bouquet garni
½ cup (125 mL) dry white wine
2 cups (500 mL) water
double quantity Herbed Yogurt Dressing *(see recipe)*

Check fish fillets for bones and set aside. Combine parsley, celery, peppercorns, bouquet garni, wine and water in frying pan. Bring to boil, reduce heat and simmer for 5 minutes.

Pour dressing into a heatproof container and stand in a bowl of very hot water. Stir occasionally so dressing heats through.

Simmer fish fillets in cooking liquid for 3–5 minutes until fish flakes with fork (cooking time depends on thickness of fillets). Drain fish and arrange on a serving plate. Spoon dressing over and serve.

Serves 10–12

Clockwise from top left: Mussels and Snow Peas; Gazpacho; Herbed Yogurt and Cucumber Soup

BAKED SNAPPER

2 x 4 lb (2 kg) whole snappers, scaled
   and cleaned
2 lemons
freshly ground pepper, to taste
6 green onions, finely chopped
1 stalk celery, finely chopped
2 tsp (10 mL) polyunsaturated oil
4 cups (1 L) whole-wheat fresh
   breadcrumbs
grated rind of 1 orange
juice of 2 oranges
salt (optional)
few sprigs fennel
extra 2 lemons (for garnish)

Grate rind of 1 lemon and set aside rind.
Squeeze 2 lemons and brush juice over
skin and inside cavity of both fish. Season
cavity with pepper and set aside for 30
minutes.

Heat oil and fry green onions and celery 3 minutes. Drain off any oil. Combine
breadcrumbs with vegetables, lemon and
orange rind and enough orange juice to
bind ingredients. Taste and adjust seasoning. Stuff fish with filling and secure
with skewers. Place sprigs of fennel on
top.

Place fish in greased baking dishes,
cover with greased foil and bake at 350°F
(180°C) for 40–60 minutes until cooked
when tested.

Remove foil and fennel and arrange
fish on serving platters. Garnish with extra
fennel and lemon wedges. Serve with
steamed seasonal vegetables and salad.

Serves 10–12

BEEF AND BROCCOLI
WITH SOY SAUCE
DRESSING

1¾ lbs (800 g) broccoli, cut in florets
   and blanched
1 lb (450 g) lean roast beef, sliced
   thinly
1 red pepper, seeded and sliced
¼ lb (110 g) mushrooms, sliced
1 cup (250 mL) bean sprouts
8 oz (225 g) can water chestnuts,
   drained and halved
freshly ground pepper, to taste
¼ cup (60 mL) white wine vinegar
¼ cup (60 mL) soy sauce
1 tsp (5 mL) grated fresh ginger
1 tbsp (15 mL) vegetable oil

In a large salad bowl combine broccoli, beef,
red pepper, mushrooms, bean sprouts and
water chestnuts; season well with pepper.
Combine remaining ingredients and pour
over salad just before serving.

Serves 6

LAMB AND VEGETABLE
KEBABS

4½ lb (2 kg) boned leg of lamb
1½ cups (375 mL) Tomato Dressing
   (see recipe)
⅔ lb (300 g) mushrooms
3 green peppers, seeded

Trim lamb of all visible fat. Cut meat into
1¼ inch (3 cm) cubes and place in a bowl
with Tomato Dressing; leave to marinate a
minimum of 4 hours. Soak wooden skewers in water to cover for at least 30 minutes. Remove meat from the marinade
and reserve the liquid. Trim mushroom
stalks and cut green peppers into pieces
the same size as the lamb. Thread lamb,
mushrooms and green peppers alternately onto drained skewers.

Grill kebabs 12–15 minutes until
cooked as liked. During cooking, turn
kebabs and brush with reserved liquid.

Serves 10–12

SPINACH ROLLS

4 dried Chinese mushrooms soaked
   in water 10 minutes
2 tsp (10 mL) vegetable oil
1 green onion, chopped
1 clove garlic, crushed
1 tsp (5 mL) grated fresh ginger
1 cup (250 mL) shredded cabbage
½ cup (125 mL) chopped celery
½ cup (125 mL) grated carrot
1 cup (250 mL) bean sprouts
¼ cup (60 mL) chopped water
   chestnuts
3 tbsp (45 mL) soy sauce
1 tbsp (15 mL) sesame oil
1 tbsp (15 mL) dry sherry
3 tbsp (45 mL) cornstarch
salt and pepper, to taste
1 bunch spinach

Remove mushroom stalks, drain and
slice. Heat oil, stir-fry mushrooms, green
onion and garlic 3 minutes. Add ginger,
cabbage, celery, carrot, bean sprouts and
water chestnuts. Cook 5 minutes.
Combine soy sauce, sesame oil and sherry; blend in cornstarch and stir into vegetables. Adjust seasonings and cook
mixture until it thickens and boils. Allow to
cool.

Wash spinach and remove hard stems.
If large, cut spinach leaves into pieces
about 5 inches (12 cm) square. If small,
use whole spinach leaves. Place 1 tbsp
(15 mL) of mixture on each spinach leaf,
roll up and seal ends. Steam rolls over
boiling water until spinach is tender. Serve
hot.

Serves 4

FRENCH ROAST
CHICKEN

2 x 3 lb (1.5 kg) chickens
2 tsp (10 mL) polyunsaturated
   margarine
3 tbsp (45 mL) water
½ lb (225 g) button mushrooms,
   chopped
5 tbsp (75 mL) chopped parsley
5 cups (1.25 L) fresh whole-wheat
   breadcrumbs
salt (optional)
freshly ground pepper, to taste
juice of 2 lemons
4 cups (1 L) Chicken Stock
   (see recipe)

Rinse and wipe chickens, discard any fat
found in body cavity, as well as neck and
giblets.

In a frying pan simmer margarine,
water and mushrooms for 5 minutes.
Cook further if necessary to allow excess
liquid to evaporate and set aside to cool.
Combine mushrooms, parsley, breadcrumbs, salt and pepper. Divide stuffing
between two chickens. Truss chickens for
roasting and preheat oven to 375°F
(190°C).

Boil chicken stock in 2 roasting pans on
top of stove. Put a rack in each dish and
arrange chickens, on their sides, on the
racks. Brush chickens with lemon juice
and cover with foil.

Roast for 20 minutes. Turn chickens
onto their other side, brush with more
lemon juice, cover with foil again and
roast a further 20 minutes.

Turn chickens onto their backs, brush
with lemon juice and roast, covered, for a
further 20 minutes. Remove foil and continue roasting, basting occasionally, until
cooked through. Turn oven off and let
chickens stand for 5 minutes before
carving.

Serves 6–8

Baked Snapper; French Roast Chicken

Slimline Salads

SALAD GREENS WITH TOMATO DRESSING

1 romaine lettuce, washed
1 Boston lettuce, washed
4 green onions, trimmed and sliced
1 green pepper, sliced
3 tbsp (45 mL) chopped parsley
⅓–½ cup (85–125 mL) Tomato
   Dressing *(see recipe)*

Tear both lettuces into pieces. Place in a salad bowl with green onions, green pepper and parsley. Toss lightly. Cover and chill until serving time. Just before serving, add dressing and toss to coat all the ingredients.

Serves 10–12

TOMATO AND GREEN PEPPER SALAD

1½ lbs (675 g) tomatoes, peeled
1 bunch green onions, thinly sliced
3 green peppers, sliced
⅓ cup (85 mL) Salad Dressing
   (see recipe)
⅓ cup (85 mL) Herbed Yogurt
   Dressing *(see recipe)*

Cut tomatoes into wedges, discarding core section. Place in a bowl with green onions and green peppers. Mix dressings together and stir into salad. Serve chilled.

Serves 10–12

FENNEL AND ORANGE SALAD

3 heads fennel
3 oranges
⅓–½ cup (85-125 mL) Tomato
   Dressing *(see recipe)*
3 tbsp (45 mL) chopped parsley

Trim fennel, slice thinly; wash well and discard any discolored slices. Cut both ends from oranges then cut off all rind and pith. With a small sharp knife, cut between membranes of oranges and free segments. Remove any seeds. Combine oranges, fennel and dressing. Cover, chill and serve sprinkled with parsley.

Serves 10–12

CAULIFLOWER AND BROCCOLI SALAD

1 lb (450 g) cauliflower
1 lb (450 g) broccoli
1 cup (250 mL) Creamy Vinaigrette
   Dressing *(see recipe)*
1–2 tsp (10 mL) Dijon mustard
1 tsp (5 mL) capers, chopped
Tabasco sauce, to taste
paprika, to taste

Wash cauliflower and broccoli and separate into florets. Cook broccoli and cauliflower separately until tender but still crisp. Drain and cool. Combine dressing with mustard, capers and Tabasco sauce. Adjust seasonings to taste. Arrange cooked vegetables in a serving dish and spoon dressing over. Cover and chill until serving time. Serve sprinkled with paprika.

Serves 10–12

BROWN RICE SALAD WITH TOMATO DRESSING

2 oranges, segmented
2 cups (500 mL) brown rice, cooked
4 green onions, sliced
1 large red pepper, diced
1 large green pepper, diced
1 cup (250 mL) Tomato Dressing
   (see recipe)
salt (optional)
freshly ground pepper, to taste

Cut rind and all pith from oranges. With a small sharp knife, cut between the membrane and flesh of each segment and free the orange flesh. Remove and discard any seeds.

Combine oranges, rice, green onions, and green and red peppers. Pour dressing over and toss lightly. Season to taste. Place in a serving bowl. Cover and chill until serving time.

Serves 10–12

Clockwise from top: Tomato and Green Pepper Salad; Salad Greens with Tomato Dressing; Cauliflower and Broccoli Salad

Dressing up

SALAD DRESSING

3 tbsp (45 mL) cornstarch
⅔ cup (165 mL) low-fat milk
1 tbsp (15 mL) prepared mustard
1 tbsp (15 mL) margarine
1 egg, beaten
3 tbsp (45 mL) vinegar
⅓ cup (85 mL) polyunsaturated oil
salt (optional)
freshly ground pepper, to taste

Mix cornstarch with a little milk. Heat remaining milk to simmering. Add cornstarch mixture, stir well and simmer until thickened. Remove from heat and stir in mustard and margarine. Beat in egg, then gradually add vinegar and oil. Return mixture to pan and heat gently until thick, stirring constantly. Do not allow to boil. Allow dressing to cool. Add seasonings. Use as directed.

Makes approximately 1¼ cups (310 mL)

HERBED YOGURT DRESSING

1 cup (250 mL) low-fat yogurt
3 tbsp (45 mL) chopped parsley
1 tbsp (15 mL) chopped chives
1 tbsp (15 mL) prepared mustard
salt (optional)
freshly ground pepper, to taste

Combine yogurt, herbs and seasonings in a bowl. Store in an airtight container and refrigerate. Use as directed.

Makes approximately 1 cup (250 mL)

FRENCH DRESSING

¼ cup (60 mL) white wine vinegar
salt and freshly ground pepper, to taste
½ tsp (2.5 mL) sugar
½ tsp (2.5 mL) dry mustard
1 clove garlic, peeled and lightly pressed
½ cup (125 mL) olive oil

Combine vinegar, salt and pepper, sugar, mustard and garlic in a screw-topped jar or blender. Shake or blend until well blended. Gradually add oil and mix until combined.

Makes ¾ cup (185 mL)

Left to right: Salad Dressing; Herbed Yogurt Dressing; French Dressing; Tomato Dressing; Creamy Vinaigrette Dressing

TOMATO DRESSING

1 cup (250 mL) tomato juice
juice of 1 lime or ½ lemon
2 green onions, finely chopped
2 cloves garlic, chopped
Worcestershire sauce, to taste
Tabasco sauce, to taste
freshly ground pepper, to taste

Combine all ingredients and mix thoroughly. Store in an airtight container in the refrigerator. Use as directed.

Makes 1 cup (250 mL)

CREAMY VINAIGRETTE DRESSING

This recipe is the basis of many fine salad dressings that add pizzazz to leafy green vegetables. To vary the flavor or add a gourmet touch, use the unique flavors of walnut or almond oil blended with a little herb or raspberry vinegar. These are all quite strong, so use sparingly and combine with vegetable oil or white vinegar to make the correct proportions.

½ cup (125 mL) white wine vinegar
salt and freshly ground pepper
1 cup (250 mL) olive oil (or a
**   combination of ½ olive oil and**
**   vegetable oil)**

Combine all ingredients in a screw-topped jar and shake.

Makes 1½ cups (375 mL)

Unforbidden Fruits

ORANGE SHERBET

10 oranges
1½ tbsp (20 mL) gelatine
3 tbsp (45 mL) water
sugar substitute, to taste
4 egg whites

Squeeze juice from oranges and strain. Sprinkle gelatine over water and leave for a few minutes to soften. Set container of gelatine in a pan of very hot water and stir until dissolved. Combine with orange juice and add sweetener to taste.

Pour mixture into a cake pan and freeze until half-frozen. Tip mixture into a bowl and beat well to break down ice crystals. Place in refrigerator.

Whisk egg whites until stiff and fold into orange juice mixture. Return mixture to freezer and freeze until half-frozen. Turn into a bowl again and beat to break down ice crystals. Refreeze. Beat once more if desired.

Note: If you own an ice cream maker, follow the manufacturer's instructions for sherbet.

Serves 10–12

CHILLED LEMON SOUFFLÉ

1½ cups (375 mL) evaporated skim milk
3 tbsp (45 mL) gelatine
5 tbsp (75 mL) water
pinch salt (optional)
grated rind and juice of 4 lemons
powdered or liquid sweetener,
   to taste
4 kiwis, peeled and sliced (optional)

Chill evaporated milk in refrigerator for 24 hours. Sprinkle gelatine over water and leave to stand for a few minutes. Place container of gelatine in hot water and stir until dissolved, then set aside.

In a large chilled bowl, whisk milk and salt until frothy. Beat in gelatine, lemon rind, juice and sweetener. The dessert should taste lemony – add more juice and rind if necessary. Pour into a serving bowl and refrigerate to set. To serve, arrange kiwi slices decoratively on top of soufflé.

Serves 10–12

SUMMER FRUIT PLATTER

Fresh fruits are a good choice for dessert as they are low in fat and salt and high in fiber. During the summer months we are lucky to have a wide variety of reasonably priced fruits available to choose from. You can use tropical fruits only, temperate fruits only, or a mixture of both. Remember to select fruit that is free from bruises and soft spots. Wash all edible skinned fruit before preparing.

TROPICAL
1 large ripe pineapple
1 ripe papaya
3 ripe mangoes
10–12 lychees (optional)

TEMPERATE FRUITS
10–12 ripe apricots
10–12 ripe plums
10–12 ripe peaches
½ –1 lb (225-450 g) cherries

MIXED FRUITS
1 lb (450 g) ripe strawberries
6 kiwis
1 cantaloupe
1 lb (450 g) seedless grapes

Tropical selection: Top and tail pineapple. With a sharp knife cut off skin, including all eyes. Halve pineapple lengthwise. Cut each half into 6 wedges then cut off core. Halve and seed papaya and cut into 12 wedges. Cut mango on each side of pit. Set aside pit section. Score the flesh on the other sections into diamond patterns. Peel lychees. Arrange fruit on a platter. Cover and chill until serving time.

Temperate Fruits: Halve apricots, plums and peaches and remove pits. Arrange all fruits on a platter. Cover and chill until serving time.

Mixed Fruits: Hull strawberries. Peel kiwis and quarter. Halve cantaloupe, remove seeds, cut into 12 wedges and pare off rind. Separate grapes into bunches. Arrange fruit on a platter. Cover and chill until serving time.

Each selection serves 10–12

MELON SALAD

1 cantaloupe
1 honeydew melon
½ watermelon
1 small bunch mint, shredded

Halve cantaloupe and honeydew melon and scoop out seeds. Cut flesh into balls or pieces using a melon baller or knife. Remove as many seeds from watermelon as possible. Cut flesh into balls or pieces.

Place all melon pieces in a serving bowl. Sprinkle mint over and stir. Cover and chill until serving time.

VARIATION
Substitute fresh ginger for mint. Cut 6–8 slices peeled ginger into strips and stir into melon.

Serves 10–12

STRAWBERRY SNOW

3 small baskets ripe strawberries
sugar substitute, to taste
3 tbsp (45 mL) gelatine
5 tbsp (75 mL) water
6 egg whites

Wash and hull strawberries, purée and sweeten to taste. Sprinkle gelatine over water and leave to stand for 5 minutes. Stand container of gelatine in hot water, stir to dissolve then stir gelatine into strawberry purée.

Whisk egg whites to form stiff peaks; fold into strawberries. Taste and adjust for sweetness. Spoon Strawberry Snow into a serving bowl. Cover and chill until serving time.

Serves 10–12

RHUBARB FOOL

2 bunches rhubarb
sugar substitute, to taste
2½ cups (625 mL) skim milk
6 tbsp (90 mL) custard powder

Trim rhubarb and cut into 2 inch (5 cm) pieces. Wash and place in a pan with enough water to cover halfway. Bring to boil, reduce heat and simmer, covered, until tender. Drain, reserving liquid. Purée fruit, adding liquid as necessary and sweeten to taste.

Place most of the milk in a pan. Combine remaining milk with custard powder and stir into milk. Bring to boil, stirring, and simmer until thick. Cool slightly. Mix custard and rhubarb, taste and adjust for sweetening. Spoon into a serving bowl. Cover and chill until serving time.

Serves 10–12

Clockwise from top: Strawberry Snow; Orange Sherbet; Chilled Lemon Soufflé

Teatime

One of the most civilized of British rituals, afternoon tea or a late-night supper is a pleasantly casual way to get together with friends and family.

The following recipes offer both traditional and innovative treats to satisfy every sweet tooth.

CUSTARD VANILLA SQUARES

¾ lb (340 g) ready-made frozen puff pastry, thawed

CUSTARD
4 cups (1 L) milk
⅔ cup (165 mL) sugar
¼ cup (60 mL) butter
1 cup (250 mL) cornstarch
1 tsp (5 mL) gelatine
1½ tbsp (20 mL) hot water
2 egg yolks, beaten
2 tsp (10 mL) vanilla

ICING
2 cups (500 mL) icing sugar, sifted
1 tbsp (15 mL) water
3 tbsp (45 mL) passion fruit pulp

Preheat oven to 425°F (220°C). Roll out pastry to 24 x 12 inch (60 x 30 cm) rectangle. Cut in half across width. Place on 2 baking trays, sprinkle with cold water and prick with fork. Stand pastry for 10 minutes then bake 12–18 minutes. Allow to cool on cake rack.

Combine 3 cups (750 mL) milk with sugar and butter in a pan. Dissolve sugar over low heat, stirring, then bring to boil. Blend remaining milk with cornstarch. Dissolve gelatine in the hot water and add to cornstarch mixture. Add cornstarch mixture to hot milk and heat, stirring until thick and smooth. Remove from heat and beat in egg yolks and vanilla. Allow to cool.

Blend icing sugar, water and passion fruit pulp. Trim pastry layers to fit jell roll pan. Spread icing over 1 layer of pastry and allow to set. Place second layer of pastry on bottom of jelly roll pan. Spread with very cool custard mixture. Top with iced pastry layer. Allow to set for 20 minutes before cutting into 2 inch (5 cm) squares to serve.

Makes 32

COCONUT PLUM FINGERS

BASE
¾ cup (185 mL) whole-wheat flour
¾ cup (185 mL) self-rising flour
¼ lb (110 g) butter
¼ cup (60 mL) granulated sugar
vanilla, to taste
1 egg
¼ cup (60 mL) milk

TOPPING
½ cup (125 mL) plum jam
1 cup (250 mL) chopped raisins
1 egg
3 tbsp (45 mL) sugar
1¼ cups (310 mL) shredded coconut

Preheat oven to 425°F (220°C). Sift flours together twice. Cream butter and sugar together. Blend in vanilla and egg. Fold in flour mixture and milk alternately. Press mixture evenly into greased 12 x 10 inch (30 x 25 cm) baking pan. Spread with plum jam and sprinkle with raisins. Combine egg, sugar and coconut. Spread carefully over top of raisins.

Bake for 10 minutes then reduce heat to 350°F (180°C) and bake another 10–15 minutes. Allow to cool in pan 10 minutes before cutting into 5 x 1 inch (2.5 cm) fingers. Allow to cool a further 5 minutes before removing from tin to cake rack to cool completely. Store in airtight container.

Makes 24

Clockwise from left: Austrian Cherry Walnut Cake; Apricot Banana Bread; Lemon Cheese Tartlets; Citrus Ring Cookies; Caramel Chelsea Bun

COFFEE CREAM CAKE

1 quantity Simple Sponge Cake batter
  (see recipe)
3 tbsp (45 mL) cornstarch
3 tbsp (45 mL) granulated sugar
3 tbsp (45 mL) instant coffee
1¼ cups (310 mL) milk
½ lb (225 g) butter
3 tbsp (45 mL) icing sugar
3 tbsp (45 mL) flaked almonds
glacé cherries

Preheat oven to 425°F (220°C). Prepare
Sponge Cake batter. Spread batter evenly into greased and lined jell roll pan. Bake
for 10–12 minutes.

Turn cake out onto wax paper and
remove lining paper. Leave to cool, then
cut into 3 even strips lengthwise.

Blend cornstarch, sugar and coffee with
3 tbsp (45 mL) milk. Heat remaining milk,
stir in cornstarch mixture and return to
heat. Bring to boil, stirring until thickened.
Place a piece of wet wax paper or plastic
wrap on the surface of 'sauce' and leave
to cool.

Cream butter and icing sugar. Beat
gradually into coffee sauce. Spread mixture over 2 of the cake layers, then sandwich together. Cover top and sides with
coffee cream and sprinkle with flaked
almonds. Decorate with piped rosettes of
coffee cream and glacé cherries.

AUSTRIAN CHERRY WALNUT CAKE

1 cup (250 mL) glacé cherries
2¼ cups (560 mL) self-rising flour
¾ cup (185 mL) butter
⅔ cup (165 mL) granulated sugar
3 eggs
¾ cup (185 mL) milk
1½ cups (375 mL) walnuts, finely
chopped
½ cup (125 mL) shredded coconut

Grease and line a 9 inch (22 cm) square
cake pan. Preheat oven to 350°F (180°C).
Halve the cherries and mix with 5 tbsp
(75 mL) of flour.

Beat butter until soft. Add sugar and
continue beating until mixture is light and
fluffy. Add eggs, one at a time, beating
well between additions.

Fold in flour and milk alternately, starting and finishing with flour. Fold in cherries, walnuts and coconut.

Spoon mixture into prepared pan and
bake for 50–60 minutes until cooked
when tested. Remove and cool on a cake
rack.

Makes 16–20 pieces

HAZELNUT SHORTBREAD

½ lb (225 g) butter
⅓ cup (85 mL) granulated sugar
1 cup (250 mL) ground hazelnuts
1⅔ cups (415 mL) all-purpose flour
¼ lb (110 g) semi-sweet baking
  chocolate
⅓ cup (85 mL) extra ground hazelnuts

Preheat oven to 350°F (180°C). Beat butter and sugar until creamy. Mix in hazelnuts and sifted flour. Put mixture into
piping bag with fluted tube and pipe
rounds into base of greased cupcake tins.
Bake for 15 minutes. Remove from cupcake tins to cake rack to cool. Melt chocolate in bowl placed over hot water and stir.
Dip each shortbread halfway into chocolate. Place on aluminum foil, sprinkle
chocolate with extra ground hazelnut,
and let chocolate set. Store in airtight
container.

Makes 25

CARAWAY SEED CAKE

2 cups (500 mL) all-purpose flour
2 tsp (10 mL) ground nutmeg
1 tsp (5 mL) baking soda
1 tsp (5 mL) baking powder
¼ lb (110 g) butter
1 tsp (5 mL) vanilla
1 cup (250 mL) granulated sugar
½ cup (125 mL) brown sugar
3 eggs
1 tsp (5 mL) caraway seeds
½ cup (125 mL) sour milk
  (see glossary)

TOPPING
5 tbsp (75 mL) sugar
1½ tsp (7.5 mL) ground cinnamon
2 tsp (10 mL) grated orange rind
¾ cup (185 mL) soft breadcrumbs
3 tbsp (45 mL) butter, melted

Preheat oven to 400°F (200°C). Sift flour,
nutmeg, baking soda and baking powder
together twice. Cream butter, vanilla and
sugars together until light and fluffy. Beat
in eggs. Fold in flour mixture and caraway
seeds, alternately with sour milk. Place
mixture into an 8 inch (20 cm) greased
and lined cake pan.

To make topping, combine all ingredients and sprinkle over top of cake. Bake
for 20–25 minutes or until cooked. Cool
on cake rack and serve.

*Left to right: Coffee Cream Cake and
Caraway Seed Cake*

78

CARAMEL CHELSEA BUN

⅓ lb (150 g) butter
½ cup (125 mL) brown sugar
¼ cup (60 mL) chopped walnuts
½ cup (125 mL) chopped glacé cherries
3½ cups (875 mL) self-rising flour
½ tsp (2.5 mL) salt
2 eggs, beaten
1¼ cups (310 mL) milk
2 tbsp (30 mL) extra butter, melted
½ cup (125 mL) sugar
2 tsp (10 mL) cinnamon
1 cup (250 mL) raisins, finely chopped

Preheat oven to 425°F (220°C). Cream 4 tbsp (60 mL) butter with all the brown sugar. Spread over base of a 9 inch (22 cm) square cake pan. Sprinkle with walnuts and cherries and set aside.

Sift flour and salt together. Work in remaining butter till mixture resembles breadcrumbs. Combine eggs and milk. Add to flour mixture to form soft dough. Knead dough lightly on floured board. Roll out to rectangle shape, ¼ inch (0.5 cm) thick.

Brush surface with melted butter. Sprinkle with sugar, cinnamon and raisins. Roll up dough from longest side to form log shape. Cut into 1 inch (2.5 cm) pieces. Place cut side down into pan. Bake 25–30 minutes until cooked. Invert onto plate to cool. Serve sliced.

APRICOT BANANA BREAD

1 cup (250 mL) chopped dried
   apricots
¼ cup (60 mL) sherry
1¼ cups (310 mL) all-purpose flour
2 tsp (10 mL) baking powder
½ tsp (2.5 mL) baking soda
¼ tsp (1 mL) salt
6 tbsp (90 mL) butter
grated rind of 1 lemon
⅔ cup (165 mL) granulated sugar
2 eggs
½ cup (125 mL) mashed banana

Preheat oven to 350°F (180°C). Soak apricots in sherry for 1 hour. Drain and discard sherry. Sift flour, baking powder, baking soda and salt together twice. Cream butter, lemon rind and sugar. Beat in eggs one at a time. Fold in fruits alternately with flour mixture. Place mixture into a greased and lined loaf pan. Bake for 1 hour or until cooked. Cool on cake rack. Ice if desired, with icing of your choice.

CITRUS RING COOKIES

1 cup (250 mL) all-purpose flour
¼ tsp (1 mL) ground allspice
⅓ lb (150 g) butter
½ cup (125 mL) granulated sugar
1 egg
grated rind of 1 lemon
1 cup (250 mL) ground almonds
2 cups (500 mL) soft breadcrumbs
1 egg yolk, beaten

ICING
2 cups (500 mL) icing sugar, sifted
3 tbsp (45 mL) lemon juice
2 oz (60 g) candied orange and
   lemon rind

Preheat oven to 400°F (200°C). Sift flour and spice together twice. Cream butter and sugar. Beat in egg and lemon rind. Fold in ground almonds and breadcrumbs to form dough. Wrap dough in plastic wrap and chill for 1 hour.

Divide dough into 30 pieces and roll each piece until 4 inches (10 cm) long. Brush ends with egg yolk and join together to form ring. Place on greased baking sheets. Bake 10–15 minutes. Remove to cake rack to cool.

Combine icing sugar and lemon juice. Ice cookies and decorate with strips of candied rind.

Makes 30

ALMOND SWEETMEATS

8 oz (225 g) ground almonds
1¼ cups (310 mL) icing sugar
⅓ – ½ cup (85-125 mL) orange-
   blossom water
4 oz (110 g) pistachio nuts, peeled
   and finely chopped
2 tbsp (30 mL) granulated sugar
extra 1¼ cups (310 mL) icing sugar
extra 4 oz (110 g) pistachio nuts,
   peeled

Combine ground almonds and icing sugar with enough orange-blossom water to form a stiff paste. Knead until smooth and allow to rest. Shape paste into small walnut-sized balls.

Using a teaspoon handle, make a small hole in each ball and fill it with combined pistachio nuts and granulated sugar. Close hole over filling and reshape. Roll balls in icing sugar and place in small paper cups. Decorate the top of each ball with a peeled pistachio nut. Serve with coffee.
Note: To peel pistachio nuts, simmer for 3 minutes, drain and slip off skins. Dry on paper towels before use.

Makes about 40

STRAWBERRY JELLY ROLLS

1 oz (28 g) package red jelly powder
1½ cups (375 mL) boiling water
1 cup (250 mL) shredded coconut

SPONGE CAKE
4 eggs, separated
2 egg yolks extra
grated rind of 1 lemon
½ cup (125 mL) granulated sugar
5 tbsp (75 mL) all-purpose flour
1 tbsp (15 mL) cornstarch

FILLING
¼ cup (60 mL) butter
¼ cup (60 mL) sugar
1 tbsp (15 mL) boiling water
1 tbsp (15 mL) milk
vanilla, to taste
1 cup (250 mL) chopped strawberries

Dissolve jelly powder in boiling water by stirring well. Refrigerate to cool but not set. Preheat oven to 425°F (220°C).

Whisk egg yolks, lemon rind and half the sugar till creamy. Whisk egg whites till stiff, add remaining sugar and fold into egg yolk mixture. Sift flour and cornstarch and fold into egg mixture.

Spread evenly in a greased and lined jell roll pan. Bake for 10–12 minutes or until cooked. Remove from oven and cover with a damp tea towel until cold.

To make filling, cream butter and sugar for 5 minutes. Gradually add boiling water, milk and vanilla, beating thoroughly. Stir in strawberries.

Turn cake out and remove lining paper. Spread with strawberry cream, cut into 12 squares and roll each one up. Dip into cold jelly, roll in coconut and place on wax paper to set.

Makes 12

PINE NUT MACAROONS

2 cups (500 mL) sugar
3 cups (750 mL) ground almonds
1 tsp (5 mL) vanilla extract
4 egg whites
1 cup (250 mL) pine nuts

In a food processor place sugar, ground almonds, vanilla and egg whites. Whirl for a minute or so, to form a smooth paste. Mix whole pine nuts into this mixture and with the help of a spoon form walnut-sized balls and place on greased cookie sheet. Bake at 325°F (160°C) for 10–12 minutes.

Serves 4–6

Clockwise from left: Apricot Banana Bread; Caramel Chelsea Bun; Citrus Ring Cookies

LEMON CHEESE TARTLETS

PASTRY
1 cup (250 mL) all-purpose flour
pinch salt
6 tbsp (90 mL) butter
squeeze lemon juice
1 egg yolk

FILLING
½ cup (125 mL) sugar
3 tbsp (45 mL) cornstarch
3 tbsp (45 mL) flour
⅔ cup (165 mL) water
2 egg yolks
grated rind of 1 lemon
3 tbsp (45 mL) butter
⅓ cup (85 mL) lemon juice

Preheat oven to 450°F (230°C). Sift flour and salt in a bowl. Rub in butter. Add lemon juice and egg yolk to form dough. Knead on lightly floured board. Roll out dough till ⅛ inch thin (3 mm). Cut with fluted cookie cutter into 2 inch (5 cm) rounds.

Line tart tins with pastry rounds. Prick base and sides of pastry shells. Bake for 8–10 minutes. Cool on cake rack. Cut pastry strips from remaining dough, twist and bake on tray for 6–8 minutes.

To make filling, combine sugar, cornstarch, flour and water. Stir over low heat until mixture simmers and thickens. Remove from heat. Add yolks, lemon rind, butter and lemon juice. Set aside to cool. Spoon lemon cheese mixture into tart shells. Decorate with pastry twist, if desired. Allow to cool completely to serve. Variation: Replace lemon cheese filling with raspberry jam or caramel-butterscotch filling.

CARAMEL-BUTTERSCOTCH FILLING
1 cup (250 mL) brown sugar
⅓ cup (85 mL) all-purpose flour
¼ cup (60 mL) cornstarch
pinch salt
4 egg yolks
2¼ cups (560 mL) milk
¼ cup (60 mL) butter
2 tsp (10 mL) vanilla
¼ cup (60 mL) golden syrup or corn
   syrup

Combine brown sugar, flour, cornstarch, and salt in a pan. Beat egg yolks and milk together and add to pan. Beat mixture till smooth. Gently heat, stirring until mixture thickens. Remove from heat. Beat in butter, vanilla and syrup. Allow to cool. Use as a tart filling.

Makes 18

Left to right: Lemon Cheese Tartlets and Hazelnut Shortbread

PETITS FOURS

2 quantities Simple Sponge Cake batter *(see recipe)*

FILLING
1¾ cups (440 mL) apricot jam
½ lb (225 g) Almond Paste
 (see recipe under Gran's Traditional Christmas Cake, p. 25)

ICING
1½ cups (375 mL) icing sugar
2–3 tbsp (30–45 mL) water
1 tbsp (15 mL) rum
food coloring

DECORATIONS
glacé cherries
chocolate sprinkles
candied coffee beans
candied violets
chopped pistachios
silver dragees

Prepare 2 quantities Sponge Cake batter *(see recipe)* and divide between 3 greased and lined jelly roll pans. Bake at 425°F (220°C) for 10–12 minutes.

Remove cakes from pans while still warm. Turn out onto clean wax paper, removing paper lining. Carefully halve each cake lengthwise, giving 6 layers. Spread each layer of cake with apricot jam. Layer cake together.

Roll out almond paste to the size of the cake. Place on top of cake. Cover with foil or wax paper, weight down with a heavy wooden board and leave for 24 hours. Cut the cake into 1½ inch (3.5 cm) squares or shapes.

Beat icing sugar with water and rum till smooth. Color icing as desired. Coat cake squares in icing. Place on cake rack to dry. Pipe decorations with remaining icing and decorate with cherries, chocolate sprinkles, etc. When dry, place each square in paper cupcake cases to serve.

Makes 28

CHERRY AND NUT STRUDEL

12 sheets filo pastry
¼ lb (110 g) butter, melted
2 lbs (1 kg) pitted cherries
¾ cup (185 mL) dried breadcrumbs
1 cup (250 mL) sugar
¼ cup (60 mL) chopped almonds
icing sugar

Preheat oven to 400°F (200°C).

Place filo pastry between 2 dry tea towels and cover with a barely damp tea towel to prevent pastry from drying out while preparing the strudel. Remove 1 sheet pastry at a time and brush with melted butter. Cover with a second sheet pastry and brush again with butter. Continue with remaining pastry, using up half the butter.

Combine cherries, breadcrumbs, sugar and almonds. Place on pastry lengthwise leaving ¾ inch (2 cm) border. Fold long edges over filling, then sides. Brush edges with butter. Roll up pastry, brushing with butter to seal ends. Place seam side down onto baking sheet. Bake for 30 minutes until browned. Remove from sheet to serving plate. Dust with icing sugar to serve.

Serves 8

CHOCOLATE NUT SQUARES

¼ lb (110 g) butter
½ cup (125 mL) brown sugar
1 tbsp (15 mL) golden syrup or corn syrup
3 tbsp (45 mL) cocoa
1 egg, beaten
½ tsp (2.5 mL) vanilla
½ lb (225 g) plain sweet cookies, crushed
½ cup (125 mL) chopped nuts (walnuts, almonds or pecans)
3 tbsp (45 mL) shredded coconut

ICING
3 oz (90 g) chocolate
4 tbsp (60 mL) water
1 tsp (5 mL) vegetable oil
2 cups (500 mL) icing sugar, sifted
¼ cup (60 mL) finely chopped nuts (walnuts, almonds or pecans)

Combine butter, sugar, syrup and cocoa in saucepan. Stir over low heat to dissolve sugar, then heat until bubbling. Remove from heat and add beaten egg and vanilla, stirring until thick. Add crushed cookies, nuts and coconut and mix well. Press mixture into greased 11 x 7 inch (28 x 18 cm) baking pan. Chill until firm.

To make icing, combine chocolate, water and oil in a bowl. Place over hot water to melt. Add icing sugar and stir well to combine. Spread chocolate icing over squares. Sprinkle with nuts. Allow icing to set before cutting into squares or fingers to serve.

Makes approximately 20

MELTING MOMENTS

¼ lb (110 g) butter, softened
⅓ cup (85 mL) granulated sugar
1 egg yolk
few drops vanilla extract
grated rind of ½ lemon
1¼ cups (310 mL) self-rising flour, sifted

BUTTERCREAM FILLING
¼ lb (110 g) butter, softened
¼ cup (60 mL) icing sugar, sifted
grated rind of ½ orange
few drops orange food coloring

Cream butter until light and fluffy. Add granulated sugar and beat until dissolved. Beat in egg yolk, vanilla extract and lemon rind. Fold in sifted flour gradually to form stiff dough. Divide dough into 20 walnut-sized balls.

Place cookie balls on greased baking sheet, flattening slightly, and spacing to allow for some spreading. Bake at 375°F (190°C) for 15 minutes. Cool on a wire rack before sandwiching cookies together with butter cream.

To make filling, cream butter, add icing sugar and beat until smooth. Add grated rind and food coloring. Spread cream on flat side of 10 cookies and sandwich together with remaining cookies.

Makes 20

Melting Moments

84

Party Drinks for All

Cocktails, punches, smoothies and fizzy fruit drinks should keep your party bubbling happily for hours. This section gives a variety of delicious beverages with and without alcohol for parties of all types and for all ages.

Non-Alcoholic Drinks

BLACKBERRY FRUIT CUP

1 lb (450 g) ripe blackberries
1 cup (250 mL) sugar
8 cups (2 L) water
juice of 1 lemon
strip of lemon rind
sherry (optional)

Boil all ingredients except sherry together for 20 minutes. Strain and chill thoroughly. Serve with 1 tsp (5 mL) sherry per glass, if desired, and ice cubes.

Makes 10 cups (2.5 L)

PASSION FRUIT PUNCH

½ cup (125 mL) sugar
½ cup (125 mL) water
1 cup (250 mL) orange juice
1 cup (250 mL) lemon juice
1 cup (250 mL) passion fruit pulp
ice cubes
24 fl oz (750 mL) bottle ginger ale
orange and lemon slices for garnish

Bring sugar and water to boil, stirring constantly. Continue to cook for 5 minutes then allow to cool. Add orange and lemon juices and passion fruit. Chill until needed. To serve, place a quantity of ice cubes in punch bowl, pour the fruit syrup over ice, pour in ginger ale and garnish with orange and lemon slices.

Makes 6 cups (1.5 L)

Strawberry Soda Whizz and Chilled Fruit Punch

LEMONADE

½ cup (125 mL) lemon juice
¼ cup (60 mL) apple juice concentrate
orange extract, to taste
ice cubes
soda or mineral water

Combine lemon juice, apple juice concentrate and orange extract. To 3 tbsp (45 mL) of mixture, add ice cubes and soda water to fill a glass.

Serves 5–6

PINEAPPLE NECTAR

1 large ripe pineapple

Peel, core and chop pineapple. In a processor, purée until smooth. Strain through fine sieve, pressing down well on pulp with back of spoon. Sealed in a jar this will keep up to 7 days in refrigerator.

Makes 3 cups (750 mL)

MANGO AND COCONUT DELIGHT

2 mangoes, peeled, seeded and roughly chopped
1 cup (250 mL) canned coconut milk
1 large lemon, juiced
½ lemon, finely grated
1 tbsp (15 mL) honey or to taste
1 tsp (5 mL) vanilla extract
1 cup (250 mL) crushed ice

GARNISH
6 slices lemon, sliced thinly
mint sprigs

Combine all ingredients and blend for 20–30 seconds until smooth and creamy. Pour into tall chilled glasses. To serve, garnish with lemon and mint.

Serves 6

PARTY PUNCH

3 tbsp (45 mL) loose black tea leaves
2½ cups (625 mL) boiling water
grated rind and juice of 3 oranges
grated rind and juice of 3 lemons
1 cup (250 mL) sugar
1 cup (250 mL) water
1 cup (250 mL) fruit syrup or cordial
pulp of 6 passion fruit
1 orange, thinly sliced
1 lemon, thinly sliced
1 lime, thinly sliced
mint sprigs
ice cubes
32 oz (1 L) bottle ginger ale
32 oz (1 L) bottle soda water

Make tea with boiling water; infuse for 5 minutes then strain and cool. Simmer grated orange and lemon rinds with sugar and water for 5 minutes. Strain into tea. Add cordial and passion fruit, then chill until needed. Empty into punch bowl, add remaining ingredients and serve.

Makes 12 cups (3 L)

WATERMELON PINEAPPLE PUNCH

3 lb (1.5 kg) piece watermelon, peeled, seeded and chopped
1¼ cups (310 mL) pineapple juice
1 cup (250 mL) lime juice
1 cup (250 mL) vodka, optional
sugar, to taste
1–2 limes, thinly sliced, to garnish

Purée watermelon in blender or food processor. Force through a fine sieve, discarding any remaining pulp. Stir in pineapple and lime juices and vodka, if using. Add sugar to taste. Chill well and serve garnished with lime slices.

Makes 6 cups (1.5 L)

STRAWBERRY SODA WHIZZ

2 cups (500 mL) pineapple juice
2 cups (500 mL) ginger ale
2 cups (500 mL) soda water
1 lb (450 g) frozen strawberries
1 cup (250 mL) lemon juice

Combine pineapple juice, ginger ale and soda water. Add strawberries (which will thaw in punch) and lemon juice. Serve chilled with cocktail umbrellas and colored straws in tall glasses.

Makes 6 cups (1.5 L)

TROPICAL SUPERWHIP

1 avocado, chopped
1 banana, chopped
¼ cup (60 mL) chopped papaya
2 tsp (10 mL) honey
2 tsp (10 mL) shredded coconut
6 fresh mint leaves
2⅓ cups (585 mL) orange juice or milk

Blend all ingredients and serve in very tall glasses, with a slice of kiwi on the side of the glass. Decorate with a cocktail umbrella or fancy straw.

Serves 4

PASSIONA PUNCH

1½ cups (375 mL) water
1½ cups (375 mL) sugar
1½ tsp (7.5 mL) cream of tartar
pulp 48 passion fruit

Boil water, sugar and cream of tartar until sugar dissolves. While still boiling add passion fruit, beating with a fork for 3 minutes to extract all the juice. Pour into bowl, mix well and bottle.

To serve, add a small quantity to a glass of water or soda water. If well corked it will keep for some time.

Makes 2½ cups (625 mL)

ICE CREAM MANGO WHIP

2 mangoes, peeled, seeded and chopped
1 cup (250 mL) milk
3 tbsp (45 mL) honey
3 drops almond extract
2 cups (500 mL) vanilla or strawberry ice cream

Combine first 4 ingredients and blend until smooth. Add ice cream and blend for 10 seconds. Serve immediately with straws and spoons.

Serves 4–6

EMERALD SMOOTHIE

½ avocado, chopped
1 tsp (5 mL) honey
1¼ cups (310 mL) milk
2 scoops vanilla ice cream
cinnamon, to garnish

Blend all ingredients in blender and serve sprinkled with cinnamon.

Serves 2

MIXED FRUIT CUP

1 papaya, peeled and seeded
2 bananas, sliced
4 cups (1 L) water
1 cup (250 mL) sugar
1 cup (250 mL) orange juice
½ cup (125 mL) lemon juice
pulp 12 passion fruit
2 x 24 oz (750 mL) bottles soda water
ice cubes

GARNISH
10 strawberries, sliced
1 orange, thinly sliced
mint leaves

Purée papaya and bananas in food processor or blender. Boil water and sugar, stirring for 8–10 minutes until sugar dissolves and thin syrup is formed. Immediately pour onto orange and lemon juices. Add puréed fruit and passion fruit. Chill until needed.

To serve, add soda water and ice cubes and garnish with strawberries, orange slices and mint leaves.

Makes 12 cups (3 L)

CHILLED FRUIT PUNCH

6 cups (1.5 L) cold tea
¾ cup (185 mL) lemon juice
2 cups (500 mL) fresh orange juice
4 cups (1 L) pineapple juice
1 cup (250 mL) sugar
2.5 quarts (2.5 L) ginger ale
ice cubes
lemon slices
strawberries, hulled
mint leaves, bruised

Combine tea, juices and sugar and chill. Add ginger ale, ice cubes, lemon slices, strawberries and mint leaves.

Makes 30 glasses

Clockwise from top: Party Punch; Ice Cream Mango Whip; Emerald Smoothie

Alcoholic Drinks

CITRUS CHAMPAGNE PUNCH

1 cup (250 mL) sugar
1¼ cups (310 mL) water
grated rind and juice of 1 orange and 1 lemon
1½ cups (375 mL) grapefruit juice
1½ cups (375 mL) pineapple juice
6 cups (1.5 L) ginger ale
1 bottle champagne or sparkling wine
ice cubes
orange and lemon slices

Dissolve sugar and water in saucepan over medium heat. Add grated rind of orange and lemon and allow to cool. Combine fruit juices and syrup and chill. Before serving, add chilled ginger ale, champagne, ice cubes and fruit slices.

Makes 20 glasses

ZESTY BLOODY MARY

2¼ cups (560 mL) tomato juice
1¼ cups (310 mL) vodka
1½ tsp (7.5 mL) Worcestershire sauce
½ tsp (2.5 mL) hot sauce
¾ tsp (4 mL) celery salt
¼ tsp (1 mL) garlic powder
juice of 3 limes or lemons
ice cubes

Mix all ingredients together, then pour over ice cubes into tall glasses.

Makes 3½ cups (875 mL)

STRAWBERRY DAIQUIRI

8 ice cubes
½ lb (225 g) strawberries, hulled
3 tbsp (45 mL) granulated sugar
6 jiggers (9 oz or 280 mL) white rum
juice of 2 limes or 1 lemon

Crush ice and place in well-chilled glasses. Blend all remaining ingredients and pour over crushed ice. Serve immediately.

Serves 4−6

Left to right: Mixed Fruit Cup; Citrus Champagne Punch; Chilled Fruit Punch

Left to right: Zesty Bloody Mary and Mango and Coconut Delight

JAMAICAN FLOAT

2 tbsp (30 mL) fresh orange juice
2 tbsp (30 mL) fresh lemon juice
2 tsp (10 mL) orgeat or maraschino liqueur
1 tbsp (15 mL) brandy
2 tbsp (30 mL) light rum
3 ice cubes

TO SERVE:
2 ice cubes
1 tbsp (15 mL) dark rum
dash grenadine

Mix first 6 ingredients, (multiplying quantities if required). Half-fill a tall chilled glass.

To serve, mix remaining 3 ingredients, float on top of prepared drink and serve garnished with a thin slice of orange.

Serves 1

ALOHA PUNCH

⅓ cup (85 mL) sugar
⅓ cup (85 mL) water
8 whole cloves
1 stick cinnamon
3 cups (750 mL) pineapple juice
3 cups (750 mL) orange juice
⅓ cup (85 mL) lemon juice
3 tbsp (45 mL) rum
32 oz (1 L) bottle ginger ale
ice cubes

Combine sugar, water, cloves and cinnamon stick and simmer for 5 minutes. Allow to cool then strain into fruit juices. Chill thoroughly. To serve, mix with rum, ginger ale and ice cubes.

Makes 10 cups (2.5 L)

SHERRIED TOMATO JUICE

¾ cup (185 mL) tomato juice
salt and pepper, to taste
dash Tabasco sauce
1 tsp (5 mL) dry sherry
Worcestershire sauce
lemon wedges, to garnish

Chill the tomato juice then season to taste with the salt, pepper and Tabasco sauce. Just before serving, stir in the sherry and a few drops of Worcestershire sauce to taste. Garnish with a thin wedge of lemon.

Makes 1 cup (250 mL)

TIPSY TOMATO COCKTAIL

3½ cups (875 mL) tomato juice
½ cup (125 mL) Bordeaux wine
½ cup (125 mL) lemon juice
salt and pepper, to taste
pinch paprika
1 tsp (5 mL) tomato paste
1 cup (250 mL) whipping cream, whipped

Mix the tomato juice with the red wine and lemon juice, then season to taste with salt, pepper and paprika.
   Stir the tomato paste into the cream. Serve the drink chilled and topped with the tomato cream. Garnish with a sprinkling of paprika.

Makes 6 cups (1.5 L)

HERBED TOMATO JUICE

3 lbs (1.5 kg) tomatoes
½ cup (125 mL) water
1 onion, sliced
1 stick celery, sliced
4 sprigs basil or 1 tsp (5 mL) dried basil
3 sprigs parsley
½ bay leaf
pinch salt
pinch paprika
dash Worcestershire sauce
1 tsp (5 mL) sherry
lemon juice

Put the tomatoes into a pan with the water, onion, celery and herbs. Simmer until the tomatoes have broken up. Strain, then season to taste with salt, paprika, Worcestershire sauce, sherry and a dash of lemon juice. Pour into a glass and chill before serving.

Makes approximately 4 cups (1 L)

MINTED TOMATO JUICE

2 cups (500 mL) tomato juice
rind and juice of ½ lemon
1 tsp (5 mL) vinegar
1 tsp (5 mL) Worcestershire sauce
dash Angostura bitters
1 tsp (5 mL) finely chopped mint
salt, pepper and nutmeg, to taste

Combine all the ingredients together and chill thoroughly. Remove the lemon rind before serving.

Makes 2 cups (500 mL)

HAWAIIAN TOMATO DRINK

1½ cups (375 mL) tomato juice
½ cup (125 mL) unsweetened pineapple juice
2 tsp (10 mL) Worcestershire sauce
1 tsp (5 mL) lemon juice
1 tsp (5 mL) rum
pinch salt
pinch cayenne pepper
mint leaves, to garnish

Combine the tomato and pineapple juices with the sauce, lemon juice and rum, then season to taste with the salt and cayenne pepper. Chill thoroughly and serve garnished with mint leaves.

Makes 2 cups (500 mL)

YOGURT TOMATO MIX

½ lb (225 g) tomatoes, cored, peeled and chopped
¾ cup (185 mL) plain yogurt
¼ tsp (1 mL) Worcestershire sauce
¼ tsp (1 mL) lemon juice
dash Angostura bitters
paprika
mint leaves, for garnish

Purée the tomatoes in a food processor or blender. Mix the yogurt, Worcestershire sauce, lemon juice and bitters, then season with a dash of paprika. Chill thoroughly and serve garnished with the mint leaves.

Makes approximately 2 cups (500 mL)

A selection of tomato-based drinks

For Your Information

Glossary of Terms

Blind baking: this refers simply to the process of baking a pie or quiche crust without a filling; the uncooked pastry is first covered with a layer of foil weighted down with baking weights such as dried beans, to prevent the crust from bulging.

Bouquet garni: a combination of herbs (usually parsley, thyme and bay leaf) tied together with string if fresh or tied into a cheesecloth bag if dried, so that they can be removed from the cooked dish before serving.

Breadcrumbs:

Soft: fresh breadcrumbs, made with one- or two-day-old bread in a blender or food processor.

Dry: commercial packaged breadcrumbs.

Cheddar cheese: most of the recipes specify aged (old, or mature) cheddar, which performs better in cooked dishes than unaged cheddar.

Five-spice powder: a Chinese spice combination of cinnamon, cloves, fennel, star anise and Szechuan peppers, available from specialty stores and in the spice section of many supermarkets.

Hoisin sauce: Chinese sauce made from onions, garlic and salted black beans. Also sold as 'black bean sauce'.

Lined cake pans: to prevent cakes from sticking or burning, the instructions often suggest greasing the pan, then lining it using greased wax paper. This step is not necessary if you use modern non-stick pans; simply oil them lightly.

Pudding cloth: a piece of clean white cotton kitchen cloth which is used to enclose pudding ingredients for steaming or boiling. You can make your own using plain white cotton or several layers of fine cheesecloth.

Self-rising flour: flour which contains a leavening agent, available in the flour section of any supermarket. You can make your own self-rising flour by adding 2 level tsp (10 mL) baking powder to 1 cup (250 mL) all-purpose flour.

Sesame oil: an aromatic oil made from sesame seeds popular in Chinese cooking. There is no substitute; if you have none, leave it out of the recipe, although the flavor will be slightly different.

Sour milk: the acid in naturally soured milk combines with baking soda to produce leavening action. You can make sour milk quickly by adding 1 tsp (5 mL) vinegar or lemon juice to each cup (250 mL) of milk.

Soy sauce: made from soya beans. Some brands are very salty, so experiment to find the one you like best.

Spring-form pan: a straight-sided cake pan with a removable base.

Tahini: a paste made from crushed sesame seeds, available from health food stores, specialty stores and many supermarkets.

Yeast: the recipes call for active dry yeast, which generally must be "proofed" by adding it to a little warm (not hot) water with sugar, and letting it stand in a warm place until frothy. If the yeast mixture does not bubble, the yeast is too old and will not work.

If you need to substitute

Fresh fruit: replace with canned.

Fresh herbs: replace with a quarter of the recommended quantity of dried herbs.

Pecans: replace with walnuts.

Cantaloupe: replace with honeydew melon.

Snapper: replace with any firm white fish such as haddock or cod.

Oven Temperatures

	Fahrenheit	Celsius
Very slow	250	120
Slow	275-300	140-150
Moderately slow	325	160
Moderate	350	180
Moderately hot	375	190
Hot	400	200
	425	220
	450	230
Very hot	475-500	250-260

Measurements

Standard Metric Measures

1 cup	=	250 mL
1 tbsp	=	15 mL
1 tsp	=	5 mL

All measurements are level

Cup Measures

1 x 250 mL cup =	Ounces	Grams
breadcrumbs, dry	4½	125
soft	2	60
butter	8¾	250
cheese, grated		
cheddar	4	110
coconut, desiccated	3	90
flour, cornstarch	4½	125
plain or self-rising	4½	125
whole-wheat	4¾	135
fruit, mixed dried	6	170
honey	12	340
sugar, granulated	7	200
icing	3½	100
moist brown	8	220
nuts	4	115

Index